PROFILES IN EXCELLENCE: UTILITY CHIEF CUSTOMER OFFICERS

Penni McLean-Conner

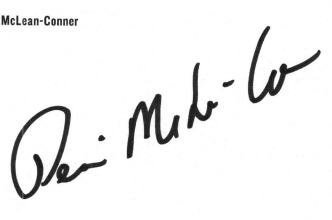

CS WEEK
Publishing
Sherman, Texas

Printed in the United States of America

Hardcover ISBN 978-0-9961360-2-0
eBook ISBN 978-0-991360-3-7

CS Week Publishing
2612 W Lamberth Rd, Ste. 300
Sherman, TX 75092
www.csweek.org
903-893-3214

To McLean and Tyler, my favorite stories begin with you.

TABLE OF CONTENTS

Foreword ix

Introduction xiii

Acknowledgments. xvii

Chapter 1: Utility Chief Customer Officers 1

Chapter 2: Marilyn Caselli, Con Edison 13

Chapter 3: Carol Dillin, Portland General Electric 35

Chapter 4: Gregory (Greg) Dunlap,
    Public Service Electric and Gas 55

Chapter 5: Joanne Fletcher, Burbank Water and Power 77

Chapter 6: Gregory (Gregg) Knight, CenterPoint Energy 97

Chapter 7: Michael (Mike) Lowe, Salt River Project 121

Chapter 8: David (Dave) McKendry, Hydro Ottawa. 143

Chapter 9: Joseph (Joe) Trentacosta,
    Southern Maryland Electric Cooperative. 163

Chapter 10: Looking Forward. 185

Author's Biography. 192

Index. 197

FOREWORD

"**B**ill Lee is a kilowatt!" It was one of the most unique affirmations I have heard someone make about a leader. The implication of this unique compliment was obviously a leader who, like a 1000 watts of power, brings light and spirit to those under his or her influence. The target of this particular declaration was the Princeton-educated CEO of Charlotte-based Duke Power, Bill Lee.

Lee was renowned in the utility industry and a pioneer in the nuclear power arena. His work forming the World Association of Nuclear Operators following Three Mile Island and Chernobyl (and serving as its first president) charted standards that govern the industry today. *Financial World* magazine named him "Leader of the Decade."

Under his leadership Duke Power morphed from largely a coal-fired and hydroelectric energy company to one with a number of nuclear plants. He also transformed the Duke culture from one that viewed customers as mere ratepayers to one that served them as valued partners. So strong was the customer first initiative that *Fortune* magazine named Duke the #1 customer service utility in the U.S. It was not surprising hundreds of Duke fans (called Dukies) would attend a rate hearing on behalf of the utility or would volunteer to serve on one of the Boards of Customers in every region of Duke's footprint.

Leaders tell a lot about themselves with interpersonal calling cards. Some leaders lead with authority—their rank or position overshadowing all other features of their resumes. Some lead with expertise—their intellectual prowess unmistakably displayed for the amazement of all they encounter. Bill Lee led with authenticity. His genuine, people-loving manner chased out any trace of fear or intimidation on the part of employees. Quality guru Edward Deming posited the first goal of an organization desiring to have quality as a priority is to "drive fear out of the workplace." Lee lived that principle.

I was a consultant to Duke for several years and worked occasionally with Bill. He was also my neighbor, living two blocks from me. Sometimes, when he walked his bulldog in front of my house and I was working in the yard, Bill would stop and we would talk as old friends. He was always curious about my consulting work. And, he was always telling stories. Like all leaders, the subject of his tales spoke volumes about his priority.

GREAT LEADERS ARE PEOPLE-CENTRIC

Bill's favorite story was one about a Duke field service tech who went to sleep in his truck while stopped at a traffic light in a residential section of Charlotte. It was during the massive cleanup following Hurricane Hugo—a storm that rolled over 200 miles inland to hit the area hard. No doubt, this field service guy had worked long hours and was exhausted. Bill's pride came through as he related how each motorist drove up behind the stopped truck, saw it was a Duke vehicle, accurately read the situation and politely maneuvered around the truck without blowing a horn, allowing its driver to catch a few more winks of much-needed sleep.

It revealed a lot about a leader more interested in being a guardian of a brand and especially the ambassadors that fronted that brand than the score-keeping numbers that delight the insatiable investor, street hungry for a financial bounty. He knew that the number one impact on customer relations was employee relations. The manner in which contact center reps, field service reps and meter readers treated customers was an echo of the way they were led. And, he demonstrated a commitment to treat them with respect, compassion and support.

GREAT LEADERS ARE CULTURE MAKERS

"No matter how visionary, brilliant, and far-reaching a leader's strategy might be," wrote entrepreneur Richard Branson, founder and CEO of Virgin Group, "it can all come undone if it is not fully supported by a strong and spirited corporate culture." To Bill Lee, 'who we want to become' was as critical a strategic decision as 'what we want to do.' Beliefs and values that resonate in the details of everyday operations must be crafted, espoused and modeled at the top. To paraphrase humorist Will Rogers, "People don't learn from conversation, they learn from observation." Bill knew employees watched his moves, not his mouth.

GREAT LEADERS GROW LEADERS

Training has always been a key part of the preparedness for most utilities. For Bill Lee, it was more than a priority; it was his passion. "Leaders don't just lead," he would tell supervisors in my classes at the company's training center on the banks of Lake Hickory, "Leaders make more leaders." To him, soft skills were as vital as hard skills, often a tough sell for analytical, 'prove-it-to-me' engineers. He never attended my classes as a visitor or an observer; Bill always stayed long enough to learn. Rosabeth Moss Kantor, best-selling author and Harvard Business School professor, affirms that approach, "Leaders are more powerful role models when they learn than when they teach."

William States Lee, III retired in 1994 and passed away from a heart attack in 1996. Then, he did not have a Chief Customer Officer; but, he clearly would have one today. However, under his leadership Duke Power (now Duke Energy) formed one of utility industries' first 24-hour customer service centers, integrating almost 100 local payment centers throughout the Duke territory. That state-of-the-art center, under the leadership of Penni McLean-Conner (and Sharon Decker), became a model for utilities around the world.

The book you hold in your hand is a goldmine of rich insights about a subject Penni Conner knows extraordinarily well. The leadership of customer service in the utility industry has emerged as a responsibility just as crucial to the welfare and longevity of an enterprise as financial acumen, engineering innovation and technological breakthroughs. At the same time, managing customer experiences and relationships has become more multifaceted and demanding. Social media has amplified customers' connections with utilities, with great service providers outside the industry having elevated their expectations.

This book will offer a powerful and pragmatic road map for bringing Bill Lee-like leadership to a quest for utility customer-centricity. The leadership profiles you will witness are instructive, insightful and inspirational. The specifics and how-to's are as cutting edge as they are practical, obviously forged in the ovens of challenging moments and complex times. This book is not a one-time drive-by read. It should be studied thoughtfully and applied compassionately.

Chip R. Bell

INTRODUCTION

A friend and colleague, Rich Charles, Partner at Ernst and Young (EY), asked me, "Why are you writing a book?" He noted that I must be very busy with two important jobs: Chief Customer Officer for Eversource Energy and Mom to thirteen- and nine-year-old sons, not to mention my involvement in various industry and community organizations. This question took me by surprise and in that moment I did not have a good answer for him. But over the next few days, I really pondered: why am I writing this book?

I know why the eight chief customer officers enthusiastically agreed to tell their stories. It is because they are passionate about customer service. And, importantly, they believe it is critical for the entire industry to advance. Utilities have enjoyed a long history of supporting each other. Think about significant storms where crews from other utilities show such a willingness to lend a hand to restore power. Utilities appreciate a unique culture that supports sharing ideas, best practices and resources.

Sharing ideas though is not easy and must be facilitated. That is where CS Week plays such a vital role. CS Week delivers with excellence on its mission to plan and deliver professional, unbiased, educational opportunities in a cost-effective manner for the electric, gas, water/wastewater utilities, cooperatives and municipalities throughout North America and the world. CS Week recognizes there exists a collective passion to take utility customer service to the next level. I am proud to work with CS Week in publishing this book. I am confident readers will gain valuable insights that will help them in their pursuit of customer service excellence.

This book was designed for aspiring utility customer service leaders: leaders with passion, leaders with energy and drive, leaders that today are already making a positive impact on utility customer service either through their roles in utility companies or in one of the many industry partners that provides valued customer service software, products and solutions.

This book was conceived by leaders like you. In 2015, at CS Week in Charlotte, NC, I pitched the concept for *Profiles* with many attendees. I was greeted with enthusiasm for the idea, which at the time I imagined would profile chief customer officers and describe how they create a customer-focused culture, discuss the customer-facing products and services they offer and learn how they develop their teams.

But what I really learned, as I vetted the concept, is that you wanted more. You wanted answers. How did these leaders arrive at or attain their chief customer officer roles? What were their career paths? How did they balance work and family? Did they experience career changing moments?

I want to thank all of you who took the time to hear me pitch the book idea and to give feedback. Because of this invaluable market research, *Profiles* explores each CCO's career path. And in my opinion, the career path discussions provide some of the most interesting and thought-provoking content in this book.

The bulk of this book features the eight individual CCO profiles. Because each CCO's profile is unique, I am proud to introduce the tool of word clouds to pictorially present each leader. A word cloud is an image composed of words used in a particular text or subject, in which the size of each word indicates its frequency or importance. In the case of these leaders, the individualized word clouds are created from interviews with them and their co-workers. This visualization tool provides strong insight into the leadership characteristics so important to a CCO.

While the profiles are fascinating, take time to also explore the opening and closing chapters. The first chapter derives the similarities across all of the chief customer officers. If you are interested in common leadership traits or best practices across all companies, then spend time absorbing this first chapter. Chapter 10, the closing chapter, is titled, 'Looking Forward.' This chapter discusses the challenges these CCOs see facing utilities and utility customer service in the future.

So why did I write this book and how would I respond to Rich's question? In the end, the answer is identical to the reason why these eight CCOs agreed to share their stories. It is because we are all passionate about our customers and customer service. We share a collective desire to take service to the next level. And we share a collective desire to help the next generation of customer service leaders achieve success in serving customers and in their personal careers.

ACKNOWLEDGMENTS

L et me just say, *Profiles* has been a fun book to write! With this effort, I was able to meet and become more deeply acquainted with eight amazing leaders, each with a unique story, strong personality and passion for their customers, their employees and their companies. The profiles at times seemed to write themselves. But the reality is, a book like this does not write itself. Rather, a published book represents the result of work and dedication and support by colleagues and family.

This is my third book. By now, my husband Nick knows the drill. He has experienced firsthand the investment writing a book takes on me and our family. Knowing that, he gave me his full support, love and encouragement all along the way. My sons, McLean and Tyler also know the drill and realize that what I need most is their love and patience, both of which they gave to me fully. My heart warms with their excitement to see this book in print.

I am honored to thank my friend, Chip Bell, having known him from my early days at Duke Power. Today, he is a renowned *New York Times* best-selling author and noted customer service expert. It is humbling to have Chip author the Foreword.

Profiles would not be in print were it not for CS Week. CS Week is a non-profit organization whose mission is to plan and deliver professional, unbiased, educational opportunities in a cost-effective manner for the electric, gas, water/wastewater utilities, cooperatives and municipalities throughout North America and the world. In

2014, CS Week Publishing was launched to offer publishing services for aspiring authors. I am proud to be the second author published and look forward to many more publications from CSWeek.

CS Week Publishing offers a great team that supports an author in so many ways. Rod Litke, CEO of CS Week, provided me with insight and candid advice throughout the process. Janet Grabinski, CS Week's copy editor, was simply amazing. She is a gifted writer in her own right and has the attention to detail so vital for copy editing. Lisa Collins headed up the marketing for *Profiles*. She planned and managed the marketing and printing of the book. Craig and Corey Sawchuk of Changed Communications developed the awesome promotional video.

I am fortunate at Eversource to work with a great team, including Margaret Norton, Director of Corporate Communications and my assistant Susan Rober. Margaret provided invaluable feedback on several portions of the manuscript, with enviable and much appreciated turnaround times. And Sue supported my writing in a variety of aspects by offering highly valued help to schedule and sometimes reschedule meetings, organizing my material and, importantly, serving as a sounding board for manuscript ideas.

Profiles tells the stories of eight accomplished utility chief customer officers. I thank and applaud each of these leaders for their success and willingness to share their pasts and presents, and even their perspectives for the future, with me. I would be remiss if I did not give voice to each profiled leader:

- Marilyn Caselli would like to thank the wonderful people at Con Edison who have given her the honor to lead, support and work side by side with them to transform the customers' experience. Marilyn gives a special shout out to Company cohorts Caroline Landau and Christopher Gallo for their assistance and guidance during the many phases of this project.

- Carol Dillin wishes to thank her wonderful colleagues at Portland General Electric who work alongside her to create a wonderful customer experience. She is also grateful

to her family's support of her career, especially her son
Jack Dillin.

- Greg Dunlap would like to thank his leadership team, Jane
Bergen, Heidi Swanson, Patricia Esler, Bill Nash, Mike Kelly
and the entire PSE&G family for their dedication and commitment to improving the customer experience. Special
thanks is offered to Karen Johnson for assisting with content
and editing and to Joe Forline for his input on the profile.
And lastly and most importantly, Greg extends a special
thank you to his wife Dr. Cherylann Dunlap for her unrelenting love and support over the past nearly 30 years.

- Joanne Fletcher offers her appreciation to Ron Davis for
his unwavering support, insightful guidance and strategic
vision which allowed her to chart new territory and spread
her wings. Joanne also extends her gratitude and affection
to her team for their loyalty, support and humor. Only
together was it possible to achieve so much.

- Gregg Knight wishes to thank the many CenterPoint
employees for their unwavering commitment to 'delivering safe and reliable energy' to millions of customers every
day. "It is through their efforts that we deliver on a brand
promise which customers, regulators and shareholders can
all take pride in. I would like to thank Alexia Dupont, David
Quin and Burke Watson on editing and telling our story."

- Mike Lowe would like to thank the board, executive team,
management staff and frontline employees at SRP who
are all so tremendously customer-focused. He especially
thanks the following members of his team for their counsel, creativity and support: Renee Castillo, Anna Lucas,
Michael Mendonca, Jim Pratt, Glen Traasdahl, Wayne
Wisdom and Cheryl Zittle.

- Dave McKendry offers his appreciation to Bryce Conrad,
Norm Fraser, Marybeth MacDonald, Michel Provost and
the entire Hydro Ottawa team, for without their vision,
guidance, passion and support, Hydro Ottawa would not

be making the headway they are creating collectively as they move from good to great.

- Joe Trentacosta wishes to thank his co-workers for agreeing to be interviewed and for their tireless support: Joe Slater for his vision and leadership, Terry Ressler for assisting with the editing process and to his wife Mary for her unwavering support of his career.

I am proud to serve on the CS Week board with Todd Arnold, Sue Daulton, Jerry Duvall, Rod Litke, Dave McKendry, Kerry Overton, Andrea Pelt-Thornton and Mark Wyatt. A few years ago, the board envisioned a way to expand on our mission of providing educational opportunities in cost-effective ways. CS Week Publishing became a reality with Todd Arnold's book, *Rethinking Utility Customer Care: Satisfying Your Always-Connected, Always-On Customers*. With *Profiles*, its second published book, CS Week continues to deliver on its mission.

Finally, I would be remiss if I did not thank you, the reader! When I was doing some market research for this book, talking with customer service leaders from across the country at CS Week in Charlotte, NC in 2015, I was greeted with enthusiastic support for the concept. In the utility industry, there is a genuine passion to drive to new levels of customer engagement and satisfaction. This demand for insights and knowledge is evidenced by the growing number of attendees each year at CS Week's annual conference. And all of you shared with me your desire to learn about how the most successful leaders in the industry created customer-focused cultures in their organizations. As you read this work, I am confident you will come away with ideas that you can use in your organizations and for your own personal development.

Writing a book is a journey, sometimes frustrating, but in the end immensely rewarding. And a published book is not possible without the tremendous support of so many people who provide their guidance, expertise, knowledge and support. If you are an aspiring author with ideas and stories to share that will enhance our utility industry, contact the CS Week Publishing team. It will be so worth it!

CHAPTER 1:
UTILITY CHIEF CUSTOMER OFFICERS

Today's utilities are laser-focused on the customer. Gone are the days when utilities referred to customers as meters or rate-payers. Indeed, the most progressive utilities engage with their consumers, a term describing all the people in a service territory using their product.

One of the most significant and visible signs of this transition by utilities to focus on customers is the increasing number of leaders who answer to the title, Chief Customer Officer (CCO). The Chief Customer Officer Council (CCO Council), a member-led, peer-advisory network, defines the role of a CCO: "An executive that provides the comprehensive and authoritative view of the customer and creates corporate and customer strategy at the highest levels of the company to maximize customer acquisition, retention and profitability."[1]

And while this title is not ubiquitous in the industry today, there are increasingly more CCOs in utilities. For example, seven years ago at the CS Week Executive Summit, Jeanne Bliss, author of *Chief Customer Officer*, met with the utility executives in attendance and asked for a show of hands of how many held the title Chief Customer Officer. In the room of 80 executives, only a handful raised their hands. Contrast that with today where, in a recent poll of CS Week attendees, 40 percent indicated their organizations had a chief customer officer.

Utility customer service leaders across the country are having a positive impact in enhancing customer experience. This impact has caught the attention of benchmarking organizations such as J.D. Power and Market Strategies International (MSI), both of which measure customer satisfaction in the utility sector.

"Energy utilities have made tremendous strides the past few years to better serve their customers," says Jeff Conklin, vice president of J.D. Power's utility and infrastructure practice. Indeed data from J.D. Power shows an overall trend of increasing customer satisfaction with the electric utility industry over the past

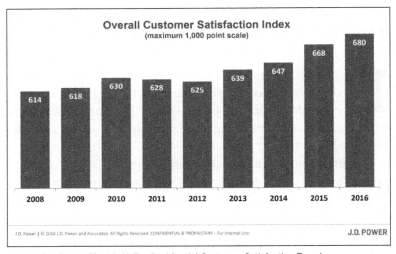

Fig. 1-1. J.D. Power Electric Utility Residential Customer Satisfaction Trend

eight years (Fig. 1-1). Jeff also adds, "One key success factor has been to leverage technology to provide consumers useful information and to create new offerings. For example, customers are delighted when their utility proactively communicates comprehensive information about an outage or when they are alerted about their energy usage and projected bill amount. Another key area of improvement has been cultural. Top performing utilities have developed a culture that puts the customer first, and they have a mindset of continuous improvement to keep up with changing customer expectations."

MSI's data on utility customer satisfaction over 20 years has also shown a steady increase in customer satisfaction across the industry. Indeed, MSI Senior Vice President Chris Oberle says, "The utility industry has optimized satisfaction through continuous quality increases in their service operations. Customer service scores for utilities are now 809 on a 1,000 point scale, and this shows how utilities are now among the top local service providers for consumers. Among 10 household service providers measured in the Market Strategies Utility Trusted Brand and Customer Engagement study, utilities rank 4th on customer ratings, just behind banks, wireless carriers and Google."

Other visible signs point the way to the increased focus on the customer in the industry as a whole. CS Week, the must-attend annual conference where utility customer service leaders network and learn about best industry practices and the latest technologies, has also transformed. Indeed, in the 1980s, it was called the CIS Users Group Conference and attracted 50 attendees, all using the same customer information system. By the 1990s, its name was updated to CIS Week, and its focus had shifted to utility customer information and enabling technology systems, with turnout rising to 800 attendees. But in the 2000s, with the name CS Week and the mission to expand excellence across the utility customer experience lifecycle, attendance is topping over 2,000.

The profiles featured in this book explore amazing utility customer leaders who all serve in the role of chief customer officer, whether that is their formal title or not (Table 1-1). Each leader has been tremendously successful in transforming utilities into customer-focused organizations. These leaders share some common leadership traits, but all have one-of-a-kind personalities they harness to drive customer strategies throughout the enterprise. And, importantly, these leaders are developing their teams and providing valued customer-facing products and services.

Table 1.1. Chief Customer Officers profiled

Name	Title	Company
Marilyn Caselli	Senior Vice President of Customer Operations	Con Edison
Carol Dillin	Vice President, Customer Strategies and Business Development	Portland General Electric
Gregory (Greg) Dunlap	Vice President - Customer Operations	Public Service Electric and Gas
Joanne Fletcher	Assistant General Manager – Customer Service & Marketing	Burbank Water and Power
Gregory (Gregg) Knight	Senior Vice President of Sales, Marketing and Customer Service & Chief Customer Officer	CenterPoint Energy
Michael (Mike) Lowe	Deputy General Manager, Customer Operations and Services & Chief Customer Executive	Salt River Project
David (Dave) McKendry	Director Customer Service	Hydro Ottawa
Joseph (Joe) Trentacosta	Senior Vice President of Customer and Enterprise Services and Chief Information Officer	Southern Maryland Electric Cooperative

CHIEF CUSTOMER OFFICER PROFILES

The eight exceptional leaders profiled in this book are all-stars in the space of utility customer service. They all reached their roles by following interesting and instructive career paths. Charged with architecting the efforts at their companies to ensure a customer-focused culture, these leaders share and embrace a relentless passion for the customer.

Of the eight leaders, only two have worked exclusively with utilities. Both Marilyn Caselli and Greg Dunlap started and continued lengthy careers at their respective utilities, Marilyn as a customer service rep and Greg as a gas engineer. Mike Lowe launched his career in the world of production planning to support a California winery, while Gregg Knight, Dave McKendry and Joe Trentacosta all worked in telecommunications. Carol Dillin interestingly began in the world of journalism, while Joanne Fletcher cut her teeth in the area of public administration.

Their careers are sprinkled with inflection points where these leaders had to reflect on core values to decide the best path forward. Some paths required physical moves across the country. The inflection points are instructive such as Dave McKendry's, whose career included moving his family around the world. But he notes, "Even magic carpet rides must come to an end." As he considered his aging parents (his children's grandparents) half-way around the world, he opted to return to Ottawa. It was an important time for his children to know their grandparents.

Mentors played a role in the careers of all these leaders, while often more informal because these leaders are indeed students of other leaders. Formal mentoring relationships also provided valuable insights to these leaders profiled.

To build the profiles out more fully, interviews were completed with the chief customer officers and folks who work with them. In this manner, insights on the leadership traits these CCOs bring to their roles were identified and graphically displayed in a word cloud. A word cloud is an image composed of words used in a particular text or subject, in which the size of each word indicates its frequency or importance. Not surprisingly, customer is the most

Fig. 1-2. Chief Customer Officer leadership traits Omni word cloud.

prominent word in the Omni cloud (Fig. 1-2) because all these leaders display a laser-focus on the customer, actively engaging their organizations to create a culture that manifests passion for the customer across all aspects of the enterprise. Fundamentally, each CCO is a great leader and, as such, cares for, engages and develops their teams and employees. These CCOs are delivering excellent customer service with investments in people, process and technology.

The customer is the passion and focus of these CCOs. These leaders possess a vision for how to serve the customer and for the customer experience (CX). Most importantly, these leaders have created a culture at their companies that aligns their processes, people and technology to deliver on the CX.

CX is prominent in the word cloud. Other words like customer-centric and customer service also show up. These CCOs are constantly thinking, talking about, engaged in understanding and enhancing the customer experience. Indeed, they have a focus, which is also large in the cloud. To do this, these leaders have defined strategies and a vision for serving customers. They actively seek, survey and listen to the voice of the customer (VoC), striving to establish a culture that delivers on the CX.

Chip Bell, *New York Times* best-selling author, describes great people-centric and committed-to-growing leaders in his foreword for this book. These CCOs are examples of outstanding leaders and each is dedicated to engaging, developing and empowering their employees. Employees and team are terms displayed really big in the cloud, closely followed by leader and develop. The word celebrate is large in the word cloud because these CCOs love celebrating success. The word collaborative is also oversized, indicative of how these leaders collaborate with business partners internally and externally to design and deliver the CX. The words coach, mentor, train, and develop also show up in the cloud.

Importantly, leadership qualities of knowledgeable, passion, credible, and integrity pop on the word cloud. Not surprisingly, each CCO brings a tremendous amount of experience to the role and a detailed understanding about customer service process, delivery and technology. While each conveys a unique perspective and style to the role, all the CCOs inherently have great leadership qualities.

Finally, there are a series of words that highlight these leaders' ability to deliver on the CX, words like technology, customer service and process. These leaders are investing in process redesign. They are defining the roadmap for their companies to achieve the customer experience vision. The roadmap includes investments in technology like advanced metering infrastructure (AMI) and smart grid. The word easy shows up too, as many of these leaders are striving to make the CX effortless. These leaders love to measure success via metrics or key performance indicators (KPIs).

CREATING A CUSTOMER-FOCUSED CULTURE

Greg Dunlap, Vice President of Customer Operations for Public Service Electric and Gas in New Jersey states his mission simply is "to establish a culture where every PSE&G employee will say they are responsible for the customer." And he stands with good company. This effort was universal among the CCOs profiled. All the CCOs have put processes in place to build or maintain a customer-focused culture. In the case of Mike Lowe, Chief Customer Executive at Salt River Project (SRP), he notes, "Ownership for the customer is a shared responsibility and customer satisfaction performance is tied to compensation for all employees."

In all cases, the CCOs shared that having support from the top for the customer was imperative. Gregg Knight, Chief Customer Officer for CenterPoint Energy, comments that their utility's entire senior executive team "has an enlightened awareness of the importance of the customer." With that foundation, Gregg has secured support and passionate engagement in the important technology investments that are transforming their customers' experience.

The CCOs have established a clear mission in regards to the customer. For some, this is built into a corporate mission; for others, the mission is inclusive of detailed descriptors of the culture, sometimes called values.

Joanne Fletcher, Assistant General Manager - Customer Service and Marketing for Burbank Water and Power (BWP), indicates that the mission provides a unifying goal for interaction and service, empowering employees to be their best. Joanne is proud that BWP's employees are "committed to exceeding customer expectations and nourishing a sustainable future for their community."

Joe Trentacosta, Senior Vice President and Chief Information Officer, shares that customer focus is part of the fiber of Southern Maryland Electric Cooperative (SMECO). As a utility co-op, SMECO is owned by its customer-members. Joe notes, "There is a laser-focus on customer service. There is no conflict on whether you are going to please the customer or the shareholder, as they are one and the same."

Carol Dillin, Vice President of Customer Strategies and Business Development at Portland General Electric (PGE) has taken the mission a step further by defining a customer's experience in the words of their customer. The intended PGE customer experience is: "In every interaction with PGE, I feel like I actually matter. It's surprising to feel genuine and authentic care from a utility, but they make me feel special...like I'm their most important customer. They're easy to do business with, any way I choose."

All these CCOs measure performance. Ron Davis, General Manager of BWP and Joanne Fletcher's boss notes, "No mission matters unless Joanne measures it." One measure that several CCOs pointed to as indicative of their culture's maturity is first call resolution. In fact, both SMECO and BWP have established goals of 100 percent first call resolution.

These CCOs pursue a relentless passion to understand what customers want and expect from their utility. The VoC is prominent in all; it is captured, analyzed and used for insights and process improvements. Several utilities are moving to leading-edge VoC tools such as online panels and voice-based analytics. The online panels provide utilities with ready access to customers to test out new ideas, communications or new functionality. Speech analytics, a sophisticated conversational analytics tool, automatically identifies, organizes and groups words and phrases spoken during calls into themes, helping to reveal rising trends and areas of opportunity or concern.

Celebrating success is a centerpiece to maintaining a culture focused on the customer. All these companies actively try to catch employees delivering great service and recognize them for their efforts. Success stories are celebrated in a variety of ways. All these CCOs personally thank employees who deliver great service. This personalized thank you can be as simple as a hand-written or emailed note to more public recognition shared amongst other employees via newsletters or even online portals. Con Edison, for example, incorporated an Applause Blog into their company Intranet. The blog, championed by Marilyn Caselli, is used to share stories about employees who provide great customer service. Selections from the blog are displayed on electronic screens throughout Con Edison's work locations.

There is also a focus on ensuring alignment of the organization and enterprise around customer service delivery and initiatives. Each CCO spends a considerable amount of time meeting with employees and employee teams, both to explore and understand progress on service delivery as well as to communicate key messages about important customer initiatives. Meetings with employees are not random though, but planned and built into the routine schedule the CCOs maintain. For example, those with represented employees have regular meetings with union leadership to share updates on initiatives and discuss important issues. Marilyn Caselli meets regularly with the union leadership at Con Ed and notes that there is a joint interest in working as collaboratively as possible, recognizing at times, "We will take positions where we agree to disagree."

All the CCOs spend time both on strategy and management of day-to-day operations. They invest considerable time reviewing metrics, performance on initiatives and VoC feedback. Their success though seems to be grounded in finding time to think strategically. Mike Lowe for example, regularly hosts his staff offsite at his cabin in the mountains of Arizona.

DEVELOPING LEADERS

All the CCOs are focused on developing leaders and their entire teams. At SRP, Mike has built this dedication to developing his team right into the mission statement: "Our employees are educated, willing and friendly. They possess the knowledge, skills and abilities to provide superior service with utmost regard for safety for all. We provide employees with targeted training and development opportunities, and we reward them with challenging work, recognition and a safe pleasant and fun work environment."

Most have very defined approaches they deploy to help customer leaders become more effective in their roles. For example, Gregg Knight, CenterPoint Energy, uses a disciplined process to systematically assess employees on both what and how they accomplish results. Talent evaluated as high in both of these categories is linked with customized developmental plans that may include cross-training or a connection with mentors.

These CCOs are using screening tools to identity the best talent to bring into the organization. They are investing in employee training. And many, like Joanne Fletcher, use a rotation of employees within the job families to build comprehensive skill sets and maintain organizational efficiency.

DELIVERING CUSTOMER-FACING PRODUCTS AND SERVICES

All the CCOs have initiatives in place or underway that will continue to transform the CX. Dave McKendry states that utility customer service comes down to seven words, "The Killer B's and All About Me." Dave explains that the Killer B's are Billing and Blackouts. And "All About Me" is really all about customers being individuals.

Old technologies are being re-invented to provide customers with 'wow' customer experiences. Take, for example, CenterPoint Energy's new interactive voice response unit (IVR). It uses natural language combined with predictive analytics to provide customers with unique and customized experiences. Today, a CenterPoint customer experiencing an outage is greeted by the IVR asking, 'Are you calling about the outage in your neighborhood?' versus IVRs of the past where customers were cautioned, 'Listen carefully as the menu options may have changed.'

Mobile-enabled service is raising the table stakes for today's always-connected customer. These CCOs are building business cases for investments in the digital presence, and customers are noticing. Beyond mobile-enabled, these companies offer downloadable applications. And in the case of PGE, they are piloting the concept of the connected home, partnering with NEST. This pilot will enable direct load control using the NEST thermostat and target addressing consumers' winter peak.

Each CCO also recognizes the customer information system (CIS) engine must be strong and robust. Some CCOs are using relatively new CIS systems, while others have legacy systems in place that continue to hum. Regardless of the age of the system, each CCO places high value on ensuring the CIS is maintained and supported with plans to ensure its health and flexibility going forward.

WRAPPING UP WITH INSIGHTS

Consistent themes emerge across these profiles, even while these leaders are designing unique customer strategies that apply to their consumers. Each leader's career path reinforces that the path is not a ladder, but rather a jungle gym grounded by individual values and welded with multiple turns and options. The culture that places a laser-focus on the customer must be shored up by shared employee responsibility. With the dramatic changes facing the utility industry, it is more important than ever that leaders are developing the next generation of utility leadership. Providing valued customer services and products must be aligned with corporate enterprise strategy.

REFERENCES

1.   Definition of Chief Customer Officer; http://www.ccocouncil.org/site/defining-the-cco.aspx. July 2016.

CHAPTER 2:
MARILYN CASELLI, CON EDISON

Many of us dream of climbing the corporate ladder, working our way up from an entry-level position to become a top executive. The reality, however, is that few will actually achieve this dream. Marilyn Caselli[1] is someone who did, and she did it in an industry traditionally dominated by men.

Marilyn began her career at Consolidated Edison Company of New York, Inc. ("Con Edison" or "the Company") in 1974, working as a customer service representative (CSR) for the utility that provides electricity, gas and steam to New York City and its northern suburb. At the time, women accounted for only 12.3 percent of the Company's 23,000 employees[2], with the majority of them working in clerical or other office positions.

Women managers were even less common. In 1978, fewer than 10 percent of Con Edison's[3] management employees were female. Nevertheless, Marilyn was promoted to a supervisory role that same year. This gave her the opportunity to showcase her leadership abilities and led to additional promotions, including one which made her the first female General Manager of Gas Operations in the Company's history.

Today, Marilyn serves as Con Edison's Senior Vice President of Customer Operations. She leads an organization of more than 2,000 employees, dedicated to delivering a low-effort, high-satisfaction customer experience. This is a task Marilyn is uniquely suited to perform. By starting at the bottom and working her way up through virtually every area of the Company, she understands how the pieces fit together and how the work Con Edison does affects the nine million New Yorkers they serve.

MARILYN CASELLI OVERVIEW

Marilyn's leadership style coalesces lessons she has learned over her 42-year career. It is informed, even today, by the four years she spent on the front line as a CSR. Marilyn's passion for the work she performs with both customers and employees and her penchant for strategic thinking are heavily reflected in her word cloud (Fig. 2-1).

Customer

To call Marilyn Caselli customer-focused would be an understatement. Even a short conversation with her reveals that the customer is positioned at the center of virtually every business decision she makes. So, it comes as no surprise that her word cloud features phrases such as CX (customer experience), VoC (voice of the customer) and customer-centric.

> "The most rewarding change is that the customer is now in the fabric of the Company."—Marilyn Caselli

The word cloud also reinforces Marilyn's belief that customer service is the responsibility of all employees; it doesn't just fall on the shoulders of Customer Operations personnel. Since 2012, she has sponsored an enterprise-level Enhancing Customer Relationships (ECR) Team, which has been tasked with training employees and ensuring the customer is a primary focus in all of the Company's operations, another word that appears frequently

Fig. 2-1. Marilyn Caselli word cloud

in her word cloud. To Marilyn, "The most rewarding change is that the customer is now in the fabric of the Company."

Employees

As a woman who has spent more than 40 years in a traditionally male-dominated industry, Marilyn understands the importance of fostering an inclusive work environment. This realization is reflected in her word cloud with words such as employee, team, engage, celebrate, leadership and women. She is proud of the progress Con Edison has made over the years in the areas of diversity and inclusion, saying, "We truly reflect the mosaic of the customers we serve, especially in Customer Operations where 75 percent are minority and female."

As a leader, Marilyn understands her responsibility to serve as a mentor to others and to encourage employees to go the extra mile. Her word cloud includes mentoring, counsel, advice and feedback. "My job is supporting people and leading change," she says, "and I make it my business to attend anything that celebrates success. It is so important that folks know how appreciative and proud we are of their work." She encourages "women to be cheerleaders for other women" and champions women's issues, including work-life balance, family and flexibility, three words which also appear prominently in her word cloud.

> "I make it my business to attend anything that celebrates success. It is so important that folks know how appreciative and proud we are of their work."— Marilyn Caselli

Strategy

Having implemented or overseen the implementation of many business processes still in place at Con Edison today, Marilyn has a personal history of delving into the details. However, she has taught herself not to wade too deeply into the weeds and instead to stay focused on strategy. This is because she believes, "Strategy is critical to create holistic alignment." Her word cloud reflects this belief with the inclusion of big picture and focus. Marilyn's leadership style is one, therefore, that provides her team with enough autonomy to run their operations, while still maintaining an appropriate level of oversight and support.

Marilyn's word cloud also includes technology, digital and AMI (advanced metering infrastructure), all of which point to the importance of technology in Con Edison's overall customer-experience strategy. Indeed, Marilyn has said, "The digital customer experience is transforming the way that we are perceived as a utility." In the near term, the Company will focus on providing its customers with greater control, choice and convenience than ever before.

UTILITY OVERVIEW: CON EDISON

Con Edison[4] is one of the nation's largest investor-owned utilities. For over 180 years, it has supplied the energy that powers New York City. The Company currently serves 3.4 million electric customers and 1.1 million gas customers in the five boroughs and Westchester County, New York's northern suburb. It manages the largest steam network in the world, providing service to over 1,600 customers. Con Edison's mission is "To provide energy services to our customers safely, reliably, efficiently, and in an environmentally-sound manner; to provide a workplace that allows employees to realize their full potential; to provide a fair return to our investors; and to improve the quality of life in the communities we service."

Recently, Con Edison has undertaken a number of initiatives designed to transform the Company and better meet the needs of its customers in the 21st century. Among other changes, it is installing smart meters capable of integrating cleaner, more efficient energy sources and completely re-envisioning its digital customer experience.

CREATING A CUSTOMER-FOCUSED CULTURE

Marilyn Caselli can recall a time when someone at Con Edison told her, "The customer experience starts and stops at the call center." Perhaps this is why she finds it so gratifying that the culture has shifted dramatically. Early in his tenure, Con Edison's Chairman and CEO John McAvoy named enhancing the customer experience as one of the Company's top three priorities, alongside safety and operational excellence. This emphasis has since been echoed over and over by Con Edison's senior leadership. Putting the customer first has become intrinsic in the way the Company conducts business. More and more, teams across the enterprise are incorporating the VoC into the way business practices, processes and technology systems are designed.

Joint Ownership of a Customer-Focused Culture

To those in other industries, it may seem odd that a company with a 180-year history is only now making a push to enhance its customer experience. But, as a regulated monopoly, Con Edison traditionally focused more on safety and reliability; it considered customer satisfaction the responsibility of one department. John McAvoy's message, however, made it clear that customer experience is one of the top priorities.

Today, Con Edison's entire leadership team has taken ownership of customer experience. Employees at all levels and positions are expected to consider the impact of their work on the people the Company serves. For Marilyn, this has been a welcome change. "In the 40 years that I have been a customer-care professional," she says, "it has been the most gratifying transformation I have seen."

Organizational Framework

Transforming the customer experience does not happen without a well-organized effort. To this end, Con Edison established the ECR Team. This Team, headed by the Customer Outreach department manager, reports directly to Marilyn. Team members represent the Company's four operating areas—Electric, Gas, Steam and Customer Operations – and includes representatives from Auditing, Law, Supply Chain and Human Resources as well.

The Team is further organized into subcommittees, each responsible for performing different functions. These include analyzing VoC data, addressing customer pain points, developing communication standards, reviewing and circulating best practices and conducting employee training, among others.

Ultimately, the Team operates in support of the philosophy shown in Figure 2-2.

> *We will examine our business through the eyes of the customer. When we identify gaps between our customers' expectations and the service that we provide, we will close these gaps wherever possible by revising our policies, procedures and practices.*
>
> *Our employees will serve as customer advocates, championing change on the customers' behalf and seeking at every touch point to provide a Plus 1 (+1) experience.*

Figure 2-2. Con Edison team philiosopy

Plus I Experiences

To effectively communicate concepts related to the customer experience, Con Edison first needed to create a common vocabulary. Marilyn championed a concept developed by Success Sciences and MG-Strategy, which focused on creating +1 customer experiences.

The +1 concept uses a simple scale that ranges from minus one to zero to plus one, based on the intersection between customers' expectations and their actual experiences.

When an experience meets a customer's expectations, it registers a zero (0) on the scale. In most cases, a score of 0 would be considered bad, but in this rating system 0 is actually a positive! For instance, Con Edison customers expect the lights will go on every time they flip a light switch. When they do, customer expectations are met—that's a 0. This experience is neither memorable to the customer nor cause for celebration, but it is satisfying nonetheless.

When the experience falls short of expectations, however, it registers as a minus one (-1). These are the types of experiences that hurt a company's reputation and foster distrust among customers.

Con Edison trains employees to identify and eliminate -1 experiences as much as possible.

Finally, +1 experiences are those in which the Company exceeds its customers' expectations. Plus 1s are memorable. They are experiences customers share with their friends and families. Plus 1s help build trust and brand loyalty. Con Edison shares stories internally and recognizes employees who seek out and deliver +1 experiences.

The +1 concept was initially communicated to all Con Edison employees via a cascade process. First, Company executives facilitated discussions with their direct reports, who then did the same with their direct reports and so on. The effort, however, did not stop there. The +1 concept has been reinforced through the creation of an Applause Blog. This Company-wide blog features customer compliments and stories of employees who have delivered +1s. Employees can also win Transforming the Customer Experience (TCX) Awards by going the extra mile to satisfy a customer's needs. As a result, +1 has become the rallying cry at the center of Con Edison's effort to create a customer-focused culture.

Investing in Customer-Facing Systems

Technology is a major component of Con Edison's strategy moving forward. The Company is investing billions of dollars to modernize its electric grid and provide customers with robust online tools to help manage their energy use. Smart meters capable of improving outage management, communicating with utility back-end systems, eliminating the need for manual meter readings and providing energy-use data in 15-minute intervals will be installed beginning in 2017. The Company is also re-envisioning its entire digital experience, developing a modern website complete with tools to give customers more control over their energy use and the associated costs. Marilyn is directly overseeing these efforts.

Marilyn realizes, however, that while technology can be transformative, it must be designed with a customer-first mentality. To achieve this focus, she has launched a comprehensive journey-mapping initiative in concert with the Digital Customer Experience (DCX) project. The initiative will be conducted by employees from across the Company to examine all of Con Edison's customer-facing processes end-to-end. The goal is to identify pain points and make the changes necessary to ensure a low-effort, high-satisfaction customer experience.

Listening to and Measuring the VoC

Incorporating VoC data into its business decisions is critical to Con Edison's ability to enhance the customer experience. To do this, the Company uses multiple tools to collect and analyze VoC data. These include key performance indicators (KPIs), surveys, focus groups, employee engagement, an online advisory community and social media.

Key performance indicators. Marilyn's organization has utilized KPIs that focus on customer experience for many years. However, at the enterprise level, these indicators have historically focused on operational and financial performance. With the Company's transformation, electric, gas and steam operations have all created KPIs based on their ability to satisfy customers' needs. Even the CEO level now holds a customer satisfaction performance indicator.

Customer surveys. Twice a year, Marilyn's organization commissions customer satisfaction surveys, which are conducted by an independent third party. This data is reviewed along with the results of nationally-syndicated research and transactional surveys to help Con Edison measure its service-delivery performance.

Customer advisory community. In 2014, Marilyn's organization worked to develop an online customer advisory community, a true game changer for gathering customer insights. More than 10,000 customers participate, a sample of their customer base that includes residential, small and large commercial and industrial customers from across Con Edison's service territory. Participants respond to quick polls and surveys and provide feedback through moderated forums. The access this community provides to VoC data has already paid dividends. Among other things, it led to the Company redesigning its electronic-billing (eBill) platform, which has since received high marks from customers.

Social media. Marilyn believes adamantly in using Twitter to gauge customer sentiment. In fact, Marilyn notes, "I read every tweet, every hour, every day. So many of the tweets provide positive feedback about our employees. But, Twitter also helps to identify service issues in real time so that they can be addressed. I look at it as a great way to get candid feedback." Her meticulous approach to reviewing every tweet that mentions Con Edison stems from her feeling that, if a customer takes time to provide feedback, it is important those comments be reviewed and understood. Her organization includes the group that responds to customer service inquiries submitted via Twitter, another enhancement designed to make it easier to do business with Con Edison.

"I read every tweet, every hour, every day."
—Marilyn Caselli

Hiring Employees with a Customer Focus

Con Edison's hiring practices reflect the Company's commitment to creating a customer-focused culture. In Marilyn's organization, perspective employees applying for customer service or customer field representative jobs are screened on their interpersonal skills, particularly their abilities to interact with customers and handle conflict.

The Company also believes in diversity and inclusion as a means of fostering a work environment that promotes respect for people from all walks of life. A statement on the Company's website reads, "The diversity of our employees reflects the diversity of the area we serve and is an essential part of Con Edison's success and strength. The many different cultures, backgrounds, languages, religions and viewpoints our workforce represents have enriched our Company's culture and made us one of the area's employers of choice."

DEVELOPING LEADERS

Marilyn knows delivering great service requires the right talent, in other words, employees who are passionate about serving others. Employees must then be organized for success, aligned in their communications and provided opportunities for growth. With this model, Marilyn has implemented quality management processes that keep her and her team focused on Con Edison's corporate values and organizational goals.

Customer Operations

Within her own organization, Marilyn has worked hard to ensure strategic alignment. Customer Operations is organized into five departments, each with its own clear set of responsibilities, objectives and performance metrics. These are Customer Assistance, Field Operations, Specialized Activities, Strategic Applications and Customer Outreach (Fig. 2-3).

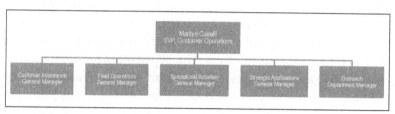

Fig. 2-3. Con Edison Customer Operations organization chart

Customer Assistance. The Customer Assistance Department ensures the Company's call center activities are efficient, timely and accurate. The team manages customer call volume and assigns resources to meet seasonal workloads, while maintaining a 24/7 telephone operation. The department responds to phone, Twitter and email-based customer inquiries. Additionally, it is responsible for designing, implementing and supporting the Company's telephony, interactive voice response (IVR) and kiosk applications.

Field Operations. The Field Operations Department plans, directs and controls Company field activities, including cycle meter reading, turn-on and turn-off requests, non-routine meter readings and collections activities. The department also handles revenue protection by identifying and correcting theft and irregular metering conditions. It maintains inactive and abandoned gas records.

Specialized Activities. The Specialized Activities Department plans, directs and controls corporate customer account activities, including billing, credit and collection, complaint handling and customer inquiries. The department completes summary and net-meter (solar) billing and manages payment options available to the Company's largest customers. Specialized Activities supports enrollment processes related to New York's competitive supply market, and it serves as a liaison for Law Department, media and governmental inquiries.

Strategic Applications. The Strategic Applications Department develops policies and rules to guide employees and customers in the migration from a regulated to a competitive energy market. In this capacity, it interacts with regulatory agencies, coordinates and designs related communications, monitors and reports on the implementation of retail access, and evaluates regulatory compliance and program effectiveness. The department provides subject matter expertise in all areas of Customer Operations and manages the online customer advisory community. Additionally, Strategic Applications provides analysis and business case development for proposed customer information system (CIS) enhancements.

Customer Outreach. Finally, the Customer Outreach Department works with the operating areas to develop outreach, educational programs and strategies to support corporate goals. As indicated by its name, the Outreach team supports a variety of customer-facing initiatives including publishing a newsletter for seniors and disabled customers, coordinating programs to assist non-English speaking and low-income customers, and serving as a liaison to social service, governmental agencies, other utilities and the New York Public Service Commission staff.

Ensuring Organizational Alignment

Alignment is important to Marilyn because it ensures various pieces of an organization, all with different responsibilities and objectives, work together to advance the Company's big-picture goals. Marilyn uses a combination of one-on-ones, staff meetings, expanded staff meetings and off-site strategy sessions to keep her organization on track and aligned.

Strategy sessions. Over the years, Marilyn has found off-site meetings valuable, as they free her staff from being distracted by the day-to-day tactical chaos. These sessions provide time to discuss organizational challenges and to brainstorm ways to create an inclusive environment that offers clear direction regarding Customer Operations' goals and objectives. Marilyn describes her approach as a cascading one in which managers are involved in developing strategies that promote operational excellence while still keeping the customer first. Marilyn candidly notes this has been a paradigm shift, recalling her early years at Con Edison when even mid-level managers simply followed directions.

Expanded staff meetings. Once each month, Marilyn hosts an expanded staff meeting, attended by over 150 Customer Operations management employees. The roster includes all her direct reports, the organization's 50 section and department managers and one-third of the frontline supervisors, who attend on a rotating basis. The meetings serve as forums for sharing important information, news about ongoing or upcoming initiatives and tips for managing the business.

One unique aspect of Marilyn's expanded staff meetings is the use of an electronic suggestion box tool, designed to create a safe environment for employees to submit questions and comments. At the end of each meeting, Marilyn reviews and addresses all submissions, reading them verbatim. She notes, "I believe people have been really pleased with our desire to be open and as transparent as possible."

Breakfast club. Marilyn typically hosts six breakfast meetings during the year, which she uses to communicate with frontline supervisors and Union employees about key issues affecting both the organization and the overall enterprise. She works to ensure these breakfast meetings represent a safe place for employees to voice issues and concerns. To this end, Marilyn deliberately prohibits section and department managers, as well as her direct reports, from participating.

Marilyn finds the breakfast clubs are a wonderful way to keep a pulse on the organization and to demonstrate her commitment to supporting employees. After each, she walks away with a wonderful laundry list of suggestions for better supporting people and ways to do things differently.

New employee orientation. Marilyn considers it a priority to meet with all new Customer Operations employees. These meetings are conducted during employee onboarding in an effort to drive home Con Edison's customer-focused culture and to provide a clear vision of the work environment that Marilyn and her team are striving to create. It is foundational to Marilyn that all new employees understand the important role they play as the face and voice of the Company.

Visibility. Visible and available to everyone in the Customer Operations organization, Marilyn promotes an open door policy, regularly visiting with field employees and meeting with Union leadership. Still, Marilyn admits, in the past, employees may have felt intimidated visiting her office. "I was upstairs from the Customer Operations folks," she explains, "on a floor that was all executive offices. I think most people felt they needed to be invited in order to come up."

In 2015, however, Marilyn took advantage of some building remodeling and moved her office to the floor occupied by Customer Outreach, Specialized Activities and Strategic Applications. "This," she notes, "was a game changer." Her employees now feel much more comfortable stopping by her office. She runs into people constantly, moving between meetings, visiting the break room or personally touching base with employees in their work spaces to celebrate a service anniversary or discuss a customer issue.

Marilyn is conscious though that the employees with whom she now shares office space make up only a fraction of her organization. There are many others, like meter readers and field employees, who spend little time in the office. Marilyn does her best to meet regularly with these employees as well. She finds a great deal of gratification in being able to speak directly with employees about their issues, successes and challenges. Of course, she also uses these opportunities to reinforce the Company's safety messaging.

Marilyn believes in promoting a cooperative relationship with the Unions that represent Customer Operations' 1,700-plus weekly employees. She meets quarterly with representatives of the Utility Workers Union of America, Locals 1-2 and 3. The approach has helped increase transparency regarding decisions that affect Union workers and has avoided an 'us versus them' mentality.

Celebrating success. Celebrating success is one of Con Edison's six core principles of *The Way We Work*[5], which also includes: plan the work and work the plan, seek and accept responsibility, work in teams, communicate openly and improve continuously. More than this, celebrating success is something in which Marilyn firmly believes. "I make it my business to attend anything that celebrates success," she says. "I think it is so important that employees know how appreciative and proud I am of their work." Indeed, Marilyn often appears unannounced at service anniversary and other recognition ceremonies, more often now that she shares a floor with many of her employees.

Career Path

Marilyn started her career in 1974 as a CSR in Con Edison's Manhattan Division. In 1978, she was promoted to a supervisory role, after which she progressively advanced through positions of increasing responsibility. She describes herself as a journeyperson, referencing her start as an entry-level employee and the subsequent jobs that took her all over the Company.

Even in the utility industry—where employees often work their entire careers for one company—finding executives who started at an entry level position is rare. This background has provided Marilyn with a real-world understanding of the life, motivations and challenges of employees at every level.

Marilyn also holds a nontraditional perspective gained from being a woman working in a male-dominated industry. Today, it is common to find female utility workers performing all manner of jobs. But when Marilyn began her career in the 1970s, more than 90 percent of Con Edison's management employees were men. Viewed through this prism, her achievements shine even more brightly, including her legacy as the first woman to serve as the General Manager in Con Edison's Gas Operations Department.

Marilyn's time in Gas Operations underscores Con Edison's commitment to leadership development and the premium that the Company places on talent who can engage and motivate the workforce. One fact Marilyn candidly admits, "When I first took the job, all I knew was the smell of gas."

This, of course, illustrates Marilyn's humility. In truth, she had established herself as a talented leader, built strong relationships within the Company and possessed transferrable business skills. These attributes, combined with the support of committed colleagues and a strong team, allowed Marilyn to quickly acclimate herself to her new role.

Grateful for the time she spent in Gas Operations and other areas of the Company, Marilyn finds innate value in having walked in the shoes of others. "It provides you with a different perspective," she says. "It helps build relationships and is an important attribute in establishing trust and respect."

After spending two years in Gas Operations, Marilyn was again promoted, becoming the Vice President of Staten Island Operations. In this role, she was responsible for overseeing all of Con Edison's work on the Island, including electric operations and customer service. This promotion made her only the second woman to run a division of the Company's Electric Operations organization.

In 1998, Marilyn assumed the role of Vice President of Con Edison's newly recentralized Customer Operations organization. She continues to serve in this role today as Senior Vice President. Despite this being her longest tenured assignment, Marilyn still finds Customer Operations both challenging and rewarding. She notes, "Not only is the industry changing, customer expectations are changing as well."

Marilyn's rise through the ranks at Con Edison was not without its challenges, however. Coincident to her promotion to general manager was the birth of her first son. At the time, there was little consideration given to work-life balance, nor was there a true appreciation of the challenges faced by working mothers and those in two-career families. Luckily, Marilyn was able to employ a wonderful caretaker to watch over her children, and her husband had a somewhat flexible work schedule. But, she understands not all women fare as fortunately.

Today, Marilyn is pleased to note how things have changed. "This is a credit to women who have demonstrated their capabilities," she proudly points out. "They've created a change in the Company's culture. I see today a lot of the younger generations are viewing life differently to create a work-life balance."

Mentors

Marilyn is a strong proponent of being a student of leadership and in mentoring to enhance leadership skills. Throughout her career, she was fortunate to receive guidance from wise and talented professionals who helped her down the right path. Three in particular gave Marilyn advice that has stuck with her even today.

Secure a Bachelor's degree. By 1978, Marilyn was already being recognized for her potential as a leader. She was promoted to a supervisory role, and her manager gave her some important advice. He urged Marilyn to make getting her degree a priority.

Based on this advice, Marilyn enrolled in State University of New York (SUNY), Empire State College and attended night and weekend classes. She completed her degree and soon realized that her timing couldn't have been better. "This was at a time," she recalls, "where it was really becoming very obvious in the utility industry that there was an anemic presence of women." Marilyn's degree put her in a position to advance, just as the industry was beginning to appreciate the value of having qualified women in the workforce.

Enhance your speaking abilities. Few accents in the world are more instantly recognizable than the Brooklyn accent. And, growing up in Bensonhurst, Marilyn was no stranger to Brooklyn-ese. She fondly describes the accent as one denoted by a tendency to swallow vowels.

Still, Marilyn never gave her accent much thought until a former Con Edison president and CEO recommended that she consider refining her speech patterns. He gently reminded her about the importance of making a good first impression and that she would likely interact more and more with those outside New York City as she continued to advance in her career. Marilyn heeded this advice and began working with a speech coach. Today, she carries just a hint of an accent, giving her an authenticity without detracting from the substance of her message.

Spend time on yourself. The third piece of advice that has resonated throughout Marilyn's career was offered by a former executive at Con Edison who was also a woman. She counseled Marilyn about the importance of putting yourself first. At the time, Marilyn had just started her family, and she welcomed the advice of a woman in a senior leadership role who also had four children of her own.

Today, Marilyn finds herself giving female employees the same advice she received. She recommends young mothers build a bit of downtime into business trips, as free and 'me' time can be very rare otherwise. She also encourages women to be cheerleaders for other women and to never compromise experience, competence, and integrity in lieu of gender.

Developing Customer Service Leadership

Marilyn recognizes that times have changed. When she started, managers felt they knew best and often dictated their employees' career paths. As Marilyn notes, "We assumed we knew best for both our customers and employees." Today, the world is very different. Customers and employees each want some level of input in the decisions that affect them. Thus, leaders must work to empower and engage their teams, preparing employees to take on different assignments.

Marilyn and her leadership team are committed to employee development. Marilyn believes in stretch assignments and challenging projects that allow employees to demonstrate their leadership skills and raise their visibility within the Company.

"One of the biggest compliments I ever received from our president," Marilyn reveals, "was that I gave my very best talent to other areas and to assignments out of my organization, so they could demonstrate their potential." Marilyn admits, at times, this generosity was offered with trepidation, but she recognizes it is critical to develop talent, and sometimes work units must sacrifice in the short term in order to gain important long-term benefits. Marilyn and her team actively look for opportunities to place talent on special assignments. She believes it is valuable to bring together employees with different perspectives to work on important projects, both for employee development and to foster an inclusive environment.

DELIVERING CUSTOMER-FACING PRODUCTS AND SERVICES

To keep pace with changing customer expectations, Con Edison is investing heavily in technology that will modernize its electric grid and provide customers with greater control, choice and convenience when managing their energy use. The Company is taking a holistic approach to developing these technologies and ensuring its decisions are based on VoC data.

Information Technology Systems

Con Edison's current CIS was first developed more than 40 years ago. Since then, it has served as the foundation for all of the Company's customer-service operations. Marilyn and her team have built a number of systems that interact with their CIS to allow it to perform tasks that could not have been envisioned in the 1970s. As a result, the system performs specialized tasks that many of today's most sophisticated platforms would struggle to replicate.

The team recognizes the Company's transition to smart meters will soon necessitate replacing their legacy CIS. But, they are proud of what they have been able to accomplish with the system that has sustained them for so long.

Initiatives in Play

An important step in Con Edison's evolution to a more customer-focused company was the launch of the My conEdison mobile app. Released for both iOS and Android devices in June 2013, the app has since been downloaded by nearly 250,000 customers.

My conEdison allows customers to complete a number of self-service functions while on the go, including:

- Viewing their billing and payment histories
- Paying their bills
- Submitting meter readings
- Locating authorized payment locations, and
- Reviewing important safety information

The app also allows the ability to report and check the status of power outages and to view the Company's online outage map.

When Con Edison first released the app, the reception was positive. The app allowed customers to perform basic transactions while on the go, and it offered a more modern and user-friendly interface than what was available on the Company's website. Recently, however, customers have indicated their expectations have changed. They want a more streamlined experience and the ability to perform a wider array of tasks, including opening an account and setting up payment agreements. These are the types of enhancements that Marilyn and her team are working to deliver through their Digital Customer Experience (DCX) project.

CX Transformation with AMI

Beginning in 2017, Con Edison intends to begin installing smart meters throughout its service territory. The project will be the largest in the Company's history and will completely transform Con Edison's business. The data provided by the smart meters and associated infrastructure will allow for improved outage management and will give customers greater control, choice and convenience in regard to their energy use.

ADVICE TO RISING LEADERS

Marilyn's advice to customer service leaders is simple: Have a relentless focus on incorporating the VoC into all that you do. Truly analyzing and understanding the VoC, she believes, is the key to developing successful short and long-term strategies.

She encourages leaders to make things happen, transform the business and influence outcomes in ways that support company objectives and provide a great customer experience. Don't just wait for things to happen, she cautions. It is critical to understand that customers' expectations are always changing, much like the customers themselves. In Marilyn's industry, customers are increasingly becoming prosumers. Prosumers are those who generate electricity in addition to consuming it. The number of customers who have solar systems and battery farms, as well as those connected to micro grids, will only increase as time goes on. It is important to recognize changes such as these as early as possible in order to develop a strategy that allows the Company to evolve.

> "Have a relentless focus on incorporating the VoC into all that you do." – Marilyn Caselli

---

Finally, Marilyn stresses the importance of fostering an inclusive workplace, where employees feel engaged and empowered to deliver +1 experiences. With this emphasis, she says, success is always possible.

REFERENCES

1.   Caselli, Marilyn. Interviewed by Penni McLean-Conner, April 11, 2016.

2.   Caselli, Marilyn. Follow up Questionnaire, May 4, 2016.

3.   Ibid.

4.   Con Edison Website; http://www.coned.com/history/; May, 2016.

5.   Con Edison 'Principles of The Way We Work;' *2012 Sustainability Report*; http://www.conedison.com/ehs/2012-sustainability-report/introduction/ ehs-policy/principles-of-the-way-we-work/index.html#gsc.tab=0

CHAPTER 3:
CAROL DILLIN, PORTLAND GENERAL ELECTRIC

In a former life, Carol Dillin[1] anchored the evening news watched by tens of thousands of television viewers in Eugene, Oregon (south of Portland). Today, she works to ensure that Portland General Electric delivers on its mission: "To be a company our customers and communities can depend on to provide electric service in a safe, sustainable and reliable manner, with excellent service, at a reasonable price."

Carol is an accomplished communicator and innovator in her persistent drive to transform the customer experience at Portland General Electric (PGE).[2] Carol has tapped into her background and training in journalism to carry forward a customer-focused culture at PGE and to effectively communicate and market services and solutions valued by its customers.

UTILITY OVERVIEW: PORTLAND GENERAL ELECTRIC

PGE has been safely and dependably powering northwest Oregon since 1889. Today, it operates a 4,000 square-mile service territory serving 840,000 customers. With its headquarters in downtown

Portland and a total of 2,600 employees,[3] PGE focuses on six pillars to ensure value is provided for all its stakeholders:

- Customer value: Keeping customers at the center of everything we do

- Environmental footprint: Protecting natural resources

- Quality workforce: Powering a safe, valued and engaged workforce

- Strong communities: Investing where we live and work

- Financial performance: Taking a long-term view

- Governance and enterprise risk management: Maintaining ethical, rigorous stewardship of our company[4]

CAROL DILLIN OVERVIEW

Carol's Director of Business Customer Group, Leslie Heilbrunn,[5] and Elizabeth Paul[6], her Director of Retail Strategy and Development, along with Carol's boss, Bill Nicholson[7], Senior Vice President, Customer Service, Transmission and Distribution, all noted Carol's passion, advocacy and persistence in delivering excellence for PGE customers. Hence, it is no surprise that customer is situated at the center of Carol's word cloud (Fig. 3-1). Carol brings to her role other important attributes, including the ability to establish vision. Her gift of storytelling supports enterprise-wide alignment around the vision. Importantly, Carol also defines the strategy and roadmap to achieve the vision in a way where the bar is set high. Carol is, at heart, an advocate for the customer and resolute in her drive to provide valued services. She is a leader who effectively engages all those around her.

Carol always places the customer as the center of focus. "The centerpiece effort of mapping customer journeys and touch points," Bill notes, "has re-invigorated the real internal focus on the customer." Leslie comments, "Carol works to ensure that all points where our employees interface with our customers result in the best experience." Additionally Bill, Leslie and Elizabeth all

Fig. 3-1. Carol Dillin word cloud

comment on the creative ways Carol safeguards that a customer focus is embedded in the culture. This included the concept of 'man on the street videos' which brought to life what customers think about PGE, what they like and what bothers them.

Carol's background in journalism and her complementary ability to clearly share a story are strong attributes she brings to PGE. She verbally paints a picture, personalizing the experience and creating a sense of urgency, all illustrative of Carol's communication skills. Indeed, Bill notes, "One of the things she does so well is sharing fantastic success stories that draw the picture of what great service is about."

A leader with high expectations, Carol also translates these communication skills into a clear strategy and roadmap. Bill shares, "Carol sets high expectations. We don't shoot for average;

rather, we strive for best in our industry and outside our industry." Leslie agrees, "Carol has really high standards and does not settle. She works internally and externally to develop solutions."

The aspect of not settling or being less than resolute in her customer advocacy was referenced often. Elizabeth shares this descriptor, "Carol is a bit of a bulldog. She is not afraid to doggedly pursue something in spite of diversity." Elizabeth shares an example of Carol's leadership to persuade the commission to allow PGE to build utility-scale green power on behalf of customers. To date, the commission has not been convinced despite strong customer outcry and request. Elizabeth notes that Carol has encouraged her team to remain undeterred and to demonstrate to PGE customers that we will keep fighting for them. Elizabeth sums it up, "Carol is the customer advocate that our customers want us to be. She has a strong passion and commitment on this subject."

Carol's focus on her team and employees was also noted, particularly in her role as a great mentor. Engaging was a term often referenced in regards to Carol's approach to leadership. Leslie notes that Carol is very engaged in projects, celebrating successes and recognizing remarkable work.

CREATING A CUSTOMER-FOCUSED CULTURE

Carol, as PGE's Vice President of Customer Strategies and Business Development, is responsible for the utility's customer-focused culture. She proudly acknowledges that ownership for creating a customer-focused culture is jointly owned. "PGE does not use the title of Chief Customer Officer," Carol explains, "because PGE recognizes it can't be just me; rather, the entire company must sign on." With Carol at the helm to build this sense of urgency, the customer remains a top priority.

"PGE does not use the title of Chief Customer Officer because PGE recognizes it can't be just me; rather, the entire company must sign on."
—Carol Dillin

The customer-focused culture is built upon the corporate strategic priorities. It starts with a defined customer experience strategy and plan and is augmented by listening to the voice of the customer (VoC), investing in customer-facing technology platforms and providing a customer-focused workspace.

Business Strategy

PGE has created a defined strategic plan to achieve their aspiration, 'Powering our customers' potential as the region's trusted energy partner.' Customers are positioned at the center of PGE's business strategy (Fig. 3.2), which has three focus areas:

1. operational excellence
2. business growth
3. corporate responsibility

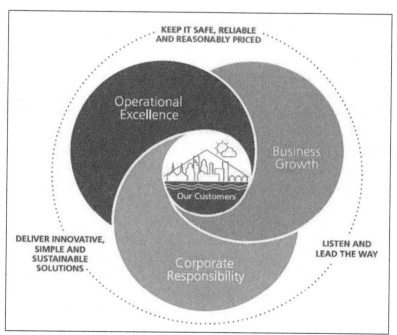

Fig. 3-2. PGE Business Strategy

Shared core principles and guiding behaviors ground PGE's business strategy. In turn, this business strategy drives the corporation's actions and initiatives.

Carol and her team led the enterprise effort to develop the strategy. Core tenets anchor the strategy's foundation: PGE provides electricity that is safe, reliability and affordable. It delivers innovative, simple and sustainable solutions. And it listens and leads the way.

Customer Experience Strategy and Plan

Carol and the PGE team are understandably proud of their tradition in providing customers with valued service. Indeed over the past few years, PGE has scored in the top 10 overall in J.D. Power rankings. It also consistently performs well as measured by customer satisfaction surveys. But as the energy marketplace and customer expectations change, the PGE team has realized that high customer satisfaction within the utility space is not enough. Customers are comparing PGE to other businesses they interact with—from local mom-and-pop shops to online behemoths like Amazon and Uber—and, as a result, they expect a more attentive, engaged and expeditious interaction with the utility.

Carol and her team take seriously the need to ensure that PGE creates meaningful, intentional customer experiences for its customers. The PGE team uses the word intentional to reference a customer experience by design. The team has created a customer experience strategy and plan to realize the goal of providing intentional customer experiences.

Creating this aligned strategy requires a thoughtful, painstaking effort, and Carol notes that to be successful it must be organic to the organization. To accomplish this alignment, Carol and her team led the enterprise through a collaborative process involving employees, leadership, customers and stakeholders. Admittedly, the process produced considerable discussion and debate, but its results shaped a strategic intent that is understood and owned by the entire enterprise.

Carol recognizes the customer strategy has to be reinforced over time. She engages external consultants to provide an outside perspective and provoke new ideas and thought. Carol is always pushing PGE to create intentional customer experiences in everything it does.

Recently, to help the enterprise think and incorporate intentional customer experiences in all they do, the strategic team created consistent messaging in the customer voice. The goal is to remind employees that, when interacting with the utility, customers want PGE to know them. One of the ways Carol accomplished this was to define the PGE experience in the words of their customers.

At PGE, the intended customer experience as shown in Figure 3-3 strives to model the following:

In every interaction with PGE, I feel like I actually matter. It's surprising to feel genuine and authentic care from a utility, but they make me feel special... like I'm their most important customer. They're easy to do business with, any way I choose. They know me when I interact with them, they actually remember my history and what I like, and they even anticipate cool things I might need. They help me make smart choices about energy in an ever-changing world. I'm impressed with PGE's commitment and advocacy for the long-term strength of our community and a sustainable future. They're a great neighbor.

Fig. 3-3. PGE's intended customer experience

Building on this focused intention, Carol and her team have identified touch points that create the PGE experience. And each touch point includes a detailed and defined description of what those experiences mean to the customer. This body of work has created the foundation upon which all initiatives are built. In all, the PGE team has identified 10 touch points:

1. Preparing to be a PGE customer
2. Starting service
3. Receiving and paying bill
4. Understanding and managing energy use
5. Powering my home or business
6. Participating in PGE programs
7. Seeing PGE in the community
8. Expanding or building home or business
9. Experiencing outages
10. Receiving PGE letter or email

For each touch point, the team has defined the intended experience. Gaps between current delivery and the intended experience have been identified and become initiatives.

VoC

Like other businesses and utilities, PGE listens to customers' voices. Using a variety of methods, PGE captures the VoC, from traditional structured phone and web surveys to collaborative approaches like focus groups and product development clinics, as well as free-form comments provided by customers on social media. Carol and her team continue to refine the process of gathering customer feedback. For example, PGE is poised to gather information via shorter surveys on key touch points to minimize the customer time involved in survey feedback. This combination of tools provides Carol and her team with a good understanding of customer concerns and performance trends.

PGE tries to understand customers' experience at both a high overall relationship level and at a very granular level. They augment the customer's voice by actively seeking input from folks who aren't direct customers but whose views and experiences help PGE serve its customers and communities better. PGE meets with industry groups such as local home builder associations to hear their perspectives and understand their current and future needs. A relationship manager works directly with each of the largest home building companies in the service territory to understand individual concerns. And all employees involved in new service connections are encouraged to share their candid feedback about how effectively PGE is implementing new tools and processes via an anonymous, online comment box.

Understanding the VoC is vital in PGE's efforts to design an intentional customer experience. PGE finds that the VoC is helpful to gain the support of operational areas in redesigning the customer experience. For example, they are currently following this model to address new service and construction work. As one of the 10 identified in the customer strategy, this touch point has taken a high priority because growth in the Portland area is booming and existing processes are stressed to meet demands. The VoC is being used to define the intentional customer experience, and gaps will be identified with remediation plans put into place.

PGE regularly and systematically measures customers' experiences, tailoring research to each customer segment, unique needs and interest. They intentionally target hard-to-reach customers to ensure many voices are heard, not just the loudest or most convenient. PGE benchmarks customer experience to past performance and against other leading utilities.

Customer-Facing Technology Platforms

Carol notes, "This is an exciting time in utility customer service delivery because of the rapid change in our industry. This excitement, though, has introduced tremendous challenges. Customers are transforming. To meet their needs, investments in processes and technology are needed."

> "This is an exciting time in utility customer service delivery because of the rapid change in our industry. This excitement, though, has introduced tremendous challenges. Customers are transforming. To meet their needs, investments in processes and technology are needed."
> —Carol Dillin

Importantly, PGE decided to invest in a technology platform that positions it to serve rapidly changing customer demands. The platform changes started with financial and field mobilization technologies. Building off this strong platform will be investments in a new customer information system (CIS) and meter data management (MDM).

Now 14 years old, the current CIS at PGE has been customized over time. When Carol and the PGE team evaluated the investments required to achieve the desired customer experiences, it became clear that an in-depth analysis of the 'as-is' CIS as compared to the 'to-be' benefits of a new CIS system needed to be completed.

Carol led this effort to build the business case. A clear corporate strategy centered on the customer plus the customer experience became the foundation and framed the business case for an investment in a replacement CIS, along with MDM.

Carol and her team recognize that implementation of customer-facing systems, such as CIS and MDM, requires a thoughtful approach. To that end, Carol is working with the entire organization to ensure customer and employee impacts are identified and well-planned.

Customer-Focused Workspace

Carol creates a customer-focused physical environment through dedicated space at PGE headquarters. In today's workplace, Carol acknowledges that employee teams often work in a virtual environment. Because employees are mobile, Carol considered the importance of creating a physical space where employees could gather and meet which also emphasized PGE's customer focus. With a series of appropriately named conference rooms like the energy partner room, Carol and her team have created a stimulating environment that is beautiful, functional and a catalyst for spurring innovation and customer-focused conversations.

DEVELOPING LEADERS

Instead of her role as PGE's Vice President Customer Strategies and Business Development, Carol's son Jack is known for teasing his mom that she could have been Oregon's own Katie Couric. Quick to reply, Carol reminds Jack that if she had been 'Oregon's Katie Couric,' then Jack would not be here embarking on his career in finance.

Indeed, Carol harbors no regrets about her career path, which started out in the world of journalism as a television anchor. She capitalized on her communications skills to move to PGE where she has flourished in public affairs and customer strategies roles for over 20 years. She has built a strong team organized for success. She is deliberate in team communications, ensuring alignment across the organization. As a constant student of leadership, Carol learns from mentors and works actively to support the development of talent within PGE.

Career Path

Carol achieved an impressive career in journalism. She combined both on-air experience in TV news with ownership of a local newspaper. This unique background demonstrates Carol's ability to design, craft and communicate key messages that inform and persuade, skillsets which Carol continues to polish in her role at PGE.

Carol's journalism career led her into television news, where she landed progressively more important reporter roles including a news anchor position in Idaho. In the world of televised reporting, progression meant moving to larger markets. Carol moved from Idaho to Oregon and was offered a role in Las Vegas. Carol had moved 11 times while still in her 20s.

At this point, Carol's career hit an inflection point, which holds true for many of the eight leaders profiled. Carol had to weigh the opportunity presented by a TV news career with the desire to grow roots in her native Portland with her husband and family. She chose Portland, and that decision became her entrée to the utility world. She joined PGE, as it afforded Carol the opportunity to further develop critical leadership skills.

Carol began working at PGE during a time when anti-nuclear sentiment was spreading across the country. In Portland, public outcry against PGE's nuclear plant was strident. Citizens organized and successfully managed to challenge the nuclear plant's continuing operation on a state-wide ballot.

PGE needed talent to manage its campaign to keep the nuclear plant open. Carol, hired as the Public Information Director, was assigned the role of designing and conducting PGE's campaign.

Carol learned a great deal about leadership during this contentious period in PGE's history. She recalls walking daily through protesters as she made her way into the office. And this antagonistic time dragged on for a couple years. Carol reflects, "The ongoing customer pushback became disheartening and unyielding for many folks, but in the end it builds character."

The campaign came to a head in the early 1990s as the public prepared to vote on this issue in the November election. Carol had spent months managing a campaign to provide balanced information, so the public could be informed for the vote. Coincidently, Carol was expecting her first child during this stressful period.

Carol tells the story of the day of the vote, November 5th. Though not due to deliver the baby until late November, she recalls feeling incredibly tired on this final vote day. She tried to put on her shoes, but they simply would not go on. In fact, her son Jack was ready to enter the scene. Instead of going home, Carol arrived at the hospital barefoot. While in labor, the final election tallies were being counted. Carol had a beautiful baby boy, and PGE won the election.

In the end, PGE shut down the plant voluntarily because the economics did not make sense. After winning such a hard fought election, PGE eventually shuttered the plant in 1993.

Carol moved into her current role as vice president customer strategies and business development in 2009. She shares, "I cannot imagine a more interesting time to contemplate strategies on how we will serve our customers. We have been providing electric service for over 100 years, but the world is changing and some customers are now partnering with us to provide their own generation. Utilities are operating in a distributed energy world, and this world is demanding collaboration with customers."

Customer Strategy and Business Development Team

With a team of over 100 people, Carol's organization includes leaders focused on new tools and customer service offerings and on managing current programs. They are responsible for customer energy solutions, including product development, program management, business development, market research, research and development and customer digital channels like the web, mobile communications and the interactive voice response (IVR) system. They also focus on energy storage options and identify new products and services that will be valued by consumers. To that end, PGE is examining micro grids, electric vehicles, high efficiency heat pumps, community solar and voluntary renewable programs, all paving the way for a future that will be electrified and decarbonized.

Carol's team also services managed accounts, PGE's largest commercial and industrial customers. In this effort, Carol's group is supported by an analytical team that completes load forecasting, marketing and digital adoption data.

Mentors

Carol has benefitted from mentoring. From a more formal approach, Carol has long enjoyed the counsel of Peggy Fowler, PGE's former CEO. Carol also gains from informal mentoring, both from thought leaders internal to PGE and external colleagues in the utility business.

One of the first women utility CEOs in the country, Peggy Fowler led PGE during the challenging years of ownership by Enron and its subsequent bankruptcy filings in the early 2000s. She returned PGE to the New York Stock Exchange in 2006 and remained CEO until 2009.

Carol learned a great deal from Peggy, recalling how generously she shared time and coaching tips on how to be successful. Peggy combined a business acumen and toughness with empathy towards people. She always spent time asking employees about their families. This personal touch is a leadership element Carol has incorporated into her own style.

Carol has found helpful counsel from folks external to the utility industry. She purposely sought out male leaders because utility leadership was historically male-dominated. These mentors and thought leaders have guided and helped Carol from a number of perspectives. She credits her mentors for encouraging her to be visible and to share her accomplishments. Carol has taken on more diverse challenges and projects to further build her skills. And advice from mentors prompted Carol to pursue a master's degree in business administration.

Ensuring Team Alignment

Carol believes in the importance of messaging and connecting with her team in multiple communication channels. She uses monthly work reviews to discuss customer initiatives and projects, along with performance metrics.

Twice a year, Carol hosts all-hands meetings. Considerable planning goes into these meetings to ensure key messages and tone are communicated effectively because the all-hands meetings combine a bit of fun with a stimulating environment, achievement celebrations and the opportunity to ensure alignment on key company initiatives.

Carol is excited to build her team with new employees, particularly those who are innovative. She strives for a team that displays a passion for creating intentional customer experiences. Because PGE is always focused on offering customers new services and options, employees joining the team need to be enthusiastic about new opportunities they can create for customers.

Talent Development

Carol and PGE take talent development very seriously. In addition to completing performance reviews, the company engages in a talent review process with the idea of supporting succession planning. The process involves individually assessing leaders, looking at their strengths and weaknesses and identifying areas of needed developmental growth. But this effort takes the next step by identifying activities to support this development. Activities like leading a project team, moving laterally to another leadership role or moving into a promotional opportunity are examples of those next encouraging steps.

DELIVERING CUSTOMER-FOCUSED PRODUCTS AND SERVICES

Intentional customer experiences is the mantra for PGE. Carol and her team have worked diligently to implement products and services that address customer pain points and offer customers new ways to manage their energy usage. Enhancing and innovating the overall customer experience focuses Carol and her team. The deliberate mapping of the 10 customer touch points laid the foundation for initiatives to enhance the experience, including an overhaul of the telephony and web channels to process payments and extensions. Carol's team continues to lead in this innovative area with a pilot deploying NEST thermostats that targets the winter peak. Recognizing the focus on cleaner transportation, PGE is also leading the way with energy solutions that include electrification of transportation.

Customer Experience Intent

"Our customers have come to expect excellent service and value from PGE," Carol recognizes, "And our technology solutions must enable us to address them. Increasingly, customers want more self-service, faster response times and easily accessible information. They ask for value-added products and demand a more personalized, interactive and consistently positive customer experience across all channels." Carol recognizes these challenges and rises to address them.

She continues, "Our technology and business process must help satisfy these expectations rather than hinder them. We must create a technology foundation that allows us to achieve the level of customer service and loyalty envisioned by PGE's Customer Experience Intent Statement, knowing customers want to do business with us in new ways that require advanced technology."

To help satisfy these needs, Carol describes the Customer Touchpoints Project to replace three mission-critical customer systems – the outdated CIS, MDM and knowledge management system. The current CIS is obsolete, built on technology created before smart metering and the demand for self-service customer offerings. Its outdated platform inhibits PGE's ability to introduce new products and services that customers desire. Similarly, their MDM, also built on aging technology, limits PGE's ability to keep pace with changes in the marketplace.

Replacing these obsolete systems with new technology will allow PGE to offer a more flexible foundation to tailor services for customers and meet their needs in a cost-effective manner. At the same time, employees need a single, user-friendly and more functional tool that helps them provide optimal service and support for customers.

According to Carol, PGE is integrating the Customer Experience Intent Statement into the systems replacement project in several ways:

- Adopting project guiding principles.

    - Customer experience with intention

    - Business operational efficiency and effectiveness

    - Employee experience and business readiness

    - IT operational efficiency and systems performance which serve as a framework for system and process design

- Assigning a designated Business Process Owner (BPO) who is responsible for ensuring each business process meets a balance between the four guiding principles.

- Dedicating a project resource who is responsible for monitoring and evaluating business process designs for alignment with PGE's Customer Experience Intent Statement and escalating issues where customer experience is being compromised.

- Developing customer experience maps in conjunction with business process maps to expose both the operational design and the customer experience design of each process.

- Developing testing and measurement approaches related to customer experience.

IVR and Web Enhancements

One of the pain points for customers was processing payment extensions. The transaction between the customer and the customer service representative (CSR) was time consuming. Knowing that PGE customers increasingly want to self-serve, PGE worked to offer a satisfying, easy credit extension process over the web and via the IVR.

The design of the self-service payment options was grounded in customer research, foundational to creating an intentional customer experience. The team used focus groups and user tests to design, build and test the specific details of how the self-service process would work on the IVR and web.

Proof that customers love this new option is in the numbers. Calls to agents for payment extensions have reduced by close to 50 percent as more and more customers choose to use the self-service options.

Customers love the new tools so much they are talking about the experience. One customer noted, "I knew I was due and was pleasantly surprised when I found I could make arrangements on the site. BRAVO!!!!! I just think that it's very helpful, very awesome that you can call and request more time {to pay}, that you can do a lot of it by computer or phone." This solution was a win-win for customers and the CSRs.

Rush Hour Rewards Pilot with NEST Thermostats

PGE is well-known for its innovativeness, and it actively engages in new technology pilots. Not surprisingly, PGE is piloting direct load control using NEST thermostats with plans to be the first utility to offer this service for winter peaking. Summer programs have already been in play, but this particular pilot targets customers to help mitigate the winter peak.

The program, 'Bring Your Own Thermostat,' seeks to enroll 3,000 to 5,000 customers and to achieve a 1 kW reduction for each household.

PGE is focusing on customers whose homes are equipped with NEST thermostats. Participating customers will receive incentives. The vision of the NEST project is to utilize existing programmable connected thermostats (PCT) and other internet-connected appliances as a source of residential demand response. The primary goal of the pilot is to demonstrate a successful program that delivers cost-effective demand response while maintaining or increasing customer satisfaction, thereby enabling the pilot to be scaled to a full program.

The campaign to recruit customers, called Rush Hour Rewards Pilot, is currently underway. Rush Hour Rewards targets 10,000 plus owners of NEST thermostats. The project which started in the fall of 2015 has successfully recruited customers, positioning PGE to test the program in the summer of 2016. PGE will use pilot results to inform scale and expansion plans.

Using NEST as a communications platform enables PGE to notify customers of an event via the customer's iPhone or digital device of choice. The NEST project taps into the fact that many customers' homes are equipped with existing internet-connected devices such as NEST thermostats capable of responding to a demand response signal. Historically, PGE would pay for the device and installation in the home. Without the need to buy or install demand response technology for customer homes, PGE's cost for residential demand response program significantly decreases, thereby increasing the value proposition for customers and the utility.

Pilots such as this help inform PGEs future product and service offerings. Wisely, this pilot will also test the practicality of collaborating with Google as a partner.

Energy Solutions

Carol and her team recognize how important it is to stay in front of customer trends. To achieve that position, Carol's team is involved in customer research and industry forums like Edison Electric Institute (EEI) and J.D. Power.

Carol notes that customers are interested in energy solutions. Tapping into that curiosity, PGE is active in educating and supporting customers on distributed generation, solar, demand response and energy efficiency. Carol leads PGE's electrification efforts which are aligned with EEI's efforts, and she chairs the EEI electrification committee.

PGE has installed electric charging infrastructure in downtown Portland at its headquarters. In true Portland style, the electric charging stations are artful and whimsical, featuring billowing baby-blue clouds. PGE worked with a graphic designer to integrate this structure into downtown Portland's unique, artistic atmosphere.

ADVICE TO CUSTOMER SERVICE LEADERS

As she accepts ongoing service challenges facing PGE, Carol takes her role seriously as a mentor and in preparing leaders. Fundamentally, Carol advises, "Leaders must be driven to always improve. We need to be critical of our own leadership. We must honestly assess processes and services being provided to customers and the tools used to deliver service. Only by taking a diagnostic view will leaders identify areas to improve." Carol notes that building leadership is evolutionary, and she emphasizes, "Being good at what we used to be is not going to sustain a leader."

> "Leaders must be driven to always improve. We need to be critical of our own leadership. We must honestly assess processes and services being provided to customers and the tools used to deliver service. Only by taking a diagnostic view will leaders identify areas to improve." —Carol Dillin

The landscape of energy service is rapidly changing, and many new players are entering. Carol feels that successful utility customer leadership must take time to understand the new players, their products and services. "Future leaders," Carol says, "will best figure out how to partner with these new players to provide customers with an even better, more satisfying experience."

REFERENCES

1. Dillin, Carol. Interviewed by Penni McLean-Conner, October 30, 2015.

2. Dillin, Carol. Follow Up to Questionnaire Responses, March 31, 2016 and April 5, 2016.

3. PGE Website; Portland General Electric Quick Facts; https://www.portlandgeneral.com/our-company/pge-at-a-glance/quick-facts

4. PGE Website; Portland General Electric Principles & Pillars; https://www.portlandgeneral.com/our-company/pge-at-a-glance/quick-facts

5. Heilbrunn, Leslie. Interviewed by Penni McLean-Conner, February 25, 2016.

6. Paul, Elizabeth. Interviewed by Penni McLean-Conner, February 9, 2016.

7. Nicholson, Bill. Interviewed by Penni McLean-Conner, April 4, 2016.

CHAPTER 4:
GREGORY (GREG) DUNLAP,
PUBLIC SERVICE ELECTRIC AND GAS

G regory (Greg) Dunlap[1] is a career Public Service Electric and Gas (PSE&G) utility guy with more than 30 years of experience, ranging from field operations to regulatory to customer operations. Besides his current position as PSE&G's Vice President of Customer Operations, Greg also pastors a local church in North Bergen, New Jersey. And he is a devoted husband to wife, Cherylann, and dad to sons, Chuck and Shaun. When asked how he can do it all, he modestly says, "When you love what you do, anything is possible."

Greg focuses on being a positive influence, whether in the context of his family, community, church or the 6 million individual PSE&G consumers in New Jersey. Some team members have referred to Greg as the 'customer experience evangelist' because of his advocacy for electric and gas consumers and his enthusiasm for celebrating positive customer experience moments. PSE&G continues to achieve high customer satisfaction ratings among customers, having been recognized by J.D. Power, PA Consulting and Market

Strategies International (MSI) for its success in delivering great service to their customers.

"When you love what you do, anything is possible."
—Greg Dunlap

Greg's formula for success is built on his being a servant leader, one who champions a culture of customer service and strives to create a supportive, nurturing environment for his team. After safety, nothing is more important to him than having the most positive customer experience possible.

PUBLIC SERVICE ELECTRIC AND GAS OVERVIEW

New Jersey's oldest and largest provider of electric and gas service, Public Service Electric and Gas serves 2.2 million electric customers and 1.8 million gas customers. That's nearly three of every four people in the state. Named 2015 Utility of the Year by *Electric Light and Power* magazine, PSE&G owns a long tradition, dating back to 1903, of providing safe, reliable electric and gas service to New Jersey consumers.[2]

Today, PSE&G is part of Public Service Enterprise Group, a publicly traded diversified energy company. In addition to being named the Utility of the Year, PSE&G was named a 2015 customer champion, one of 13 combined gas and electric utilities in the nation to receive this honor, by Cogent Reports, a division of MSI. This group of utilities achieved top tier engaged customer relations (ECR) scores based on feedback from more than 52,000 residential customers. Three core components—brand trust, operational satisfaction and product experience—compose the overall ECR score. PSE&G ranked highest in brand trust.[3]

GREG DUNLAP OVERVIEW

Greg's colleagues provide perspectives on his leadership. Included in the interviews were Jane Bergen, Director of Billing, Revenue and

Controls; Joe Forline, Vice President Gas Operations; Bill Nash, Director of Customer Contact; and Heidi Swanson, Director of Customer Service and Large Customer Support.[4,5,6] The word cloud (Fig. 4-1) reveals several themes that describe Greg. His passion for the customer is first and foremost, but built upon this passion is Greg's leadership style, his focused delivery of excellent service and his commitment to his team.

Fig. 4-1. Greg Dunlap word cloud

Passion for Customer

Greg's passion for the customer emerges strongly in the word cloud. Other words used to describe Greg's passion include customer experience, identified as CX, and voice of the customer or VoC. His colleagues credit Greg with establishing a variety of customer listening posts that support PSE&G's solid grounding in the voice of the customer. Heidi credits Greg, "He is the champion within the organization for the customer experience. He spearheads customer experience initiatives." Bill adds, "Greg is very focused on the VoC and uses a variety of listening posts." These listening posts include J.D. Power, 'moment of truth,' executive complaints and customer compliments, among others. Bill identifies the power of compliments and how Greg shares positive stories with employees to show his appreciation for their efforts and to convince skeptics that they can do this also.

Words and phrases that describe Greg's leadership style include credible, servant leader, persuasive, pastor and ability to teach through stories. Greg's colleagues quickly point out that Greg is a full-time pastor in addition to his role as vice president. "His ability," Jane notes, "to preach the gospel extends beyond his church community to PSE&G, where the gospel is manifested by the focus on the customer." Joe, having worked with Greg for over 30 years, describes him as "a leader who demonstrates the highest integrity, works collaboratively with teammates and simply is a great role model." Joe notes, "Greg is a servant leader who shares power and places the needs of others first." Bill describes Greg's leadership style, "Credibility is a powerful trait Greg trades on as a leader. When people believe in you and believe you actually care about them, they follow. This is Greg's foundational strength as a leader."

Recognized for his knowledge and leadership, Greg focuses on delivering on customer expectations. Words used to describe this focus on delivery include focused, expectation, J.D. Power, KPI, process and relentless. Joe commends his colleague, "Greg has reduced costs to serve customers, while increasing satisfaction every year, by deliberately analyzing processes to make them more efficient and enhance the experience."

Greg is employee-focused, and the word cloud prominently illustrates this with the words engage, help, develop, support, collaborative and celebrate. Heidi notes, "Greg likes to engage folks directly and asks for their opinion." Joe expands on this point, "Greg creates forums where he can listen and interact with employees." And Greg enjoys celebrating success. Heidi shares, "When there is something to celebrate, Greg stands side by side with field crews or office staff. Greg celebrates success along the way."

CREATING A CUSTOMER-FOCUSED CULTURE

Customer focus has long been the battle cry for PSE&G. Greg's role, to champion this focus and drive the customer experience, starts by changing the conversation from customers to consumers. PSE&G has established multiple customer listening posts, organized to mine customer data for accountability and improvement. PSE&G uses both MSI and J.D. Power for measuring customer satisfaction. Additionally, PSE&G employs 'moment of truth' transactional surveys and ad-hoc online panel surveys as key customer listening posts. Key metrics focusing on the customer, including J.D. Power's survey results, are part of the overall PSE&G balanced scorecard. As a performance-driven organization, PSE&G measures for success in delivering customer service. It is continually scanning inside and outside the utility industry for customer experience tools, technologies and practices that deliver positive results.

Driving Customer Experience

At PSE&G, Greg understands his role is to be the customer experience advocate, a mantle of responsibility he wears proudly. As Vice President of Customer Operations, Greg drives a customer-centric culture via the meter-to-cash process and leads the customer satisfaction improvement process.

Greg unabashedly admits to being both a cheerleader and a badger when it comes to the customer. He is recognized at PSE&G for encouraging others to question initiatives, plans and decisions from the customer's unique perspective. "We have an opportunity to change how our customers perceive us with each interaction, no matter how small," he says. "And I really want each of our employees to think and act that way."

Greg readily confesses he is on a mission to establish a culture where all PSE&G employees will say they are responsible for the customer relationship. Achievement characterizes PSE&G's culture, and employees proudly point to safety as an example. Greg says, "Whether an employee is an administrative assistant, gas operations technician or accountant, if you ask who is responsible for safety, the response will be, 'I am.'" Safety is clearly job Number 1. By extension, Greg continues, "I want to move PSE&G's 7,200 employees to have the same focus and ownership for the customer. We have made progress, but frankly we are not there yet."

"We have an opportunity to change how our customers perceive us with each interaction, no matter how small. And I really want each of our employees to think and act that way."
—Greg Dunlap

An important way to help accomplish this task is by celebrating success to reinforce positive behaviors. Since becoming the leader of PSE&G's Customer Operations team, Greg has required every meeting to start with two foundational messages. First, all meetings kick off with a safety message, followed secondly by a customer experience story. Managers and directors typically share a story about an associate going above and beyond expectations to address a customer need, followed by public acknowledgement of the employee. In 2015, when J.D. Power ranked PSE&G highest in customer satisfaction with business natural gas service and large business electric service in the East, Greg, with two trophies in tow, visited nearly all of PSE&G's field locations to personally thank associates for their efforts. What appeared to be a modest recognition effort turned into one of the most effective ways to help associates understand how they can personally contribute to improving customer satisfaction.

Modeling this focus starts with Greg and his leadership team. To effect change, efforts and emphasis had to begin with Customer Operations. When Greg initially took on the leadership role for

Customer Operations, he mailed a letter to each associate, speaking about the opportunity each person has with every customer experience to give the customer a reason to smile or have a better outlook on the day (Fig. 4-2). Greg reminds his team that when working with a customer, they do not have control or even understand the difficulties or challenges the customer may have been dealing with before or after the interaction with the utility. But, each employee is empowered to provide that customer with a valuable experience that could potentially have a far reaching positive impact, well beyond their interaction with PSE&G. This customer-centric mentality and focus allows Greg to nurture this positiveness in Customer Operations and spread it throughout all of PSE&G.

Customers as Partners and Consumers

When Greg started in the gas and electric business 30 years ago, utility language focused on meters and ensuring the meter-to-cash operation functioned like a high quality cash register. The reference to meters then turned to ratepayers, but today's idiom is grounded in customers. Greg, though, is still not satisfied, and he challenges PSE&G to go one step further. "PSE&G serves more than 2.2 million electric and 1.8 million gas customers based on the number of accounts," he says. "When you consider the number of people in households and businesses, we actually serve about 6 million individual consumers—each with individual needs and perceptions of the service we provide. We shouldn't concentrate solely on the person who pays the utility bill. This distinction represents a potentially fundamental shift in how we think about our business model and our current and future product and service offerings."

Greg's earlier work in the public policy arena for PSE&G gave him a deep understanding of the importance of customers as partners and advocates on the company's behalf. During deregulation of the electric and gas industries, Greg witnessed how positive customer perceptions about PSE&G led to public policy that provided opportunities for the utility to expand service offerings in areas like energy efficiency and renewables. Also, when a move-

Commitment to Making a Difference

When I was in elementary school, my dream was to change the world. I had visions of becoming President of the United States, a great leader like Martin Luther King, Jr., or a great inventor like Thomas Edison. I would have even settled with becoming some sort of super hero, like Superman, who could eradicate all the bad guys! I just wanted to make the world a better place! Well, I can't tell you how disappointing it was to discover that there was a big difference between getting an "A" in Science, or being a member of the Student Council, and achieving the accomplishments of some of my childhood heroes. (And despite many attempts, I was never able to fly like Superman!) I suppose many of us had big dreams as children.....

As I grew up, my dream never changed. I still wanted to change the world. I still wanted to make the world a better place. However, what *did* change is my understanding of what it takes to make a difference. It is true that the accomplishments of great men and women have certainly changed the world. But real change, the change that matters, doesn't come just from people we read about in history books. It also comes from people just like you and me. Looking back at my childhood dream to change the world, it never occurred to me that I had the power to start making changes immediately...And when I started working at PSE&G, it didn't initially occur to me that my dream could come true!

At PSE&G, we have the opportunity to make the world a better place. We have the opportunity to make communities better...to make households better...to make people feel better! How? Every time we interact with a customer, every time we knock on a customer's door, or work in someone's neighborhood, our interaction can make a difference! The way we interact with people can change how they feel and, in turn, how they may treat others. If we have positive interactions with customers (and it's all about the customer experience!), just maybe our example will lead others to have positive interactions with people... and before you know it...we are all changing the world! My experience is that good service, good etiquette, good manners, and showing respect are contagious. We all need to remember that every interaction with a customer is our opportunity to change the world. It's our opportunity to make the world a better place...*one person at a time!* If just doing a little bit extra, being a bit more attentive, showing a bit more care and compassion, is all it takes to make someone smile, why not do it?

I understand that we all have limitations as to what we can do, but that doesn't mean we can't find ways to create a better customer experience and start changing the world...so let's do it!

In my new role as VP – Customer Operations, I'm looking forward to continuing to change the world with all of you. Under Joe Forline's leadership, we've made great strides, and now is not the time to slow down! The world is changing...customer expectations are changing...the challenges before us are changing, but together we can be a force to ensure it is all positive change!

Looking forward to working with you all!

Fig. 4-2. Greg Dunlap letter to Customer Operations employees.

ment swept the country to eliminate utilities from providing appliance repair services, New Jersey consumers instead reacted with support for PSE&G's efforts to remain in this business space. Today, PSE&G proudly operates a highly successful and robust appliance service business, able to allay service challenges primarily because of consumer support.

Greg led PSE&G efforts, including coordination with labor unions, consumer groups, and other utilities across the country, to develop policy positions and effective messaging. But most importantly, Greg learned that the customer's voice proved to be the most critical one in positioning PSE&G to continue offering this service. "Our customers made it known to legislators and regulators that PSE&G should continue this business," he recalls. This high level of customer trust continues to position PSE&G to provide services beyond electric and gas delivery.

Meeting Changing Customer Expectations

Today's consumers expect to interact differently with their utility company. Recent storms like Hurricane Irene and Superstorm Sandy reinforced customers' dependency on electricity to power everything from their mega-screen TVs to all their personal electronic devices.

"If there's one thing this extreme weather taught us, it's that customers expect their power to be on all the time," Greg says. "Customers not only want excellent reliability, they want increased resiliency against storms and other events that can interrupt their service. PSE&G developed its Energy Strong program to harden our electric and gas systems in direct response to what customers were telling us they expect." Energy Strong is a $1.22 billion program to protect PSE&G electric and gas systems against severe weather. The investment involves raising or relocating switching and substations, modernizing gas mains and deploying smart grid technologies to create redundancy in the system, among other initiatives.[7]

"Listening to our customers—and providing the products and services they expect—must be how we do business."—Greg Dunlap

---

In addition to greater resiliency, customers expect the utility of the future to deliver cleaner energy, like solar, and energy efficiency improvements. They expect service offerings to be available to all customers, not exclusively for those who can afford rooftop solar panels or a high-efficiency furnace or air conditioner. They also want their bill to remain affordable. "Listening to our customers— and providing the products and services they expect—must be how we do business," Greg says.

Customer Listening Posts

PSE&G has implemented well-established customer listening posts. These enable the utility to integrate customer perspectives into all aspects of the business, including measurement of overall PSE&G success. Listening posts include traditional surveys over multiple channels, as well as an agile online customer panel. Data collected on customer complaints and regulatory inquiries complements the surveys. Social media is actively monitored.

PSE&G uses a variety of customer survey tools, including VoC perception surveys and customer transactional surveys. PSE&G partners with J.D. Power and MSI to support the perception survey processes. Transactional surveys are managed internally by PSE&G.

Consumer perception tracking. In 2014, PSE&G switched its methodology for measuring and tracking consumer perception to J.D. Power in four areas:

1. electric residential customer satisfaction,
2. gas residential customer satisfaction,
3. electric business customer satisfaction,
4. gas business customer satisfaction.

PSE&G also uses a research firm to survey business customer satisfaction to tap into large business customers who are not surveyed by J.D. Power.

PSE&G uses the J.D. Power key driver model for each customer segment to help understand different factors impacting perception and then prioritizes improvements for the most impact. J.D. Power provides an interactive index calculator, a diagnostic simulator that supports what-if analytics. It also employs a benchmarking database that includes most of the utilities in the nation to compare data to any company or peer group across the country.

Transactional surveys. PSE&G manages a large portfolio of transactional surveys to measure customer satisfaction with their processes and to assist in making improvements. Transactional surveys include call center, walk-in center, electric and gas distribution field service, appliance service repair and emergencies, tree trimming, constituent satisfaction and water heater installation.

Online panel. Interestingly, PSE&G also uses an online panel called Power Talk, created in 2013. Power Talk provides a rapid way of gathering high-quality input from a representative group of customers to help drive business decisions at all levels. The 5,000-member panel, composed of mostly residential and a limited number of small business customers who reside within PSE&G's gas and electric territory, is engaged on strategic and operational topics. Participation is strictly voluntary, yet PSE&G has already received a high participation rate of responses to the surveys offered throughout the year. The panel members help PSE&G better understand energy trends and issues and gain valuable feedback on ways to better service its customers.

PSE&G has also used the online panel to determine whether its communications are effectively generating awareness and reaching customers through various messaging. Working jointly, the marketing, advertising and customer assessment teams developed an online panel survey to test 16 campaign marketing messages to gauge awareness and favorability. The survey results showed that infrastructure improvement, safety, and energy cost-saving messages increased customer favorability, while corporate citizenship and community involvement were less impactful to the PSE&G brand. Using the survey results, PSE&G's communications campaigns for 2016 strive to strengthen customer perceptions in these key areas. The utility also used the online panel for customer feedback on the PSE&G bill and to aid in its redesign. The panel members identified areas of importance on the bill, such as amount due and payment date, and provided feedback on how and where those items should appear. The panel's input was used to design an entirely new bill, currently being tested with focus groups and due to be implemented next year.

Organizing to Support a Customer-Centric Culture

Support for a customer-centric culture starts at the top. PSE&G has established a customer satisfaction improvement steering committee of executive leadership headed up by Ralph LaRossa, PSE&G President and Chief Operating Officer (COO). This steering team meets quarterly to review progress on customer satisfaction metrics and planning improvements. Recently, Greg formed the Customer Experience Advisory Council, which includes a few members of the senior leadership team and key business partners from Corporate Communications, Corporate Responsibility, and Information Technology.

To support the steering committee, Greg established a dedicated team, led by Patti Esler, Manager of Customer Assessment. Patti and her team manage customer satisfaction and customer experience process improvement initiatives, ensuring that the utility is listening to the voice of the customer.

Meeting monthly with a working group composed of representatives from every part of the utility business and key partners, this team is responsible for creating and implementing the customer satisfaction plan.

Measuring Success

PSE&G measures its performance using a scorecard approach. The corporate scorecard is organized into quadrants: people, safe and reliable, economic and green. The people quadrant includes metrics on employees such as diversity and engagement. Safety and reliability features measurements on employee safety and the operational performance of the gas and electric system. The economic quadrant reviews the financial metrics. And the green quadrant incorporates measures on sustainable and green initiatives in the utility.

With 29 measures in the four quadrants, 10 of them impact incentive compensation for all non-bargaining unit associates. Two-thirds of the measures on the scorecard are directly related to the customer.

"It's been said that what gets measured, gets done," Greg affirms. "I believe it is critical to link the focus on the customer with strong metrics that align employee actions with what is right for customers. This is foundational and provides motivation for employees to succeed."

> "It's been said that what gets measured, gets done. I believe it is critical to link the focus on the customer with strong metrics that align employee actions with what is right for customers. This is foundational and provides motivation for employees to succeed."
> —Greg Dunlap

Keeping Informed on Best Practices

When asked about how he stays abreast of best practices in the utility industry, Greg quips, "I call Penni from Eversource Energy." But on the serious side, Greg believes in keeping up with industry best practices and those from other industries.

To ensure the team stays current, an analyst on the team provides a monthly customer intelligence report that summarizes new utility product and service offerings, best practices and the latest trends. This intelligence report is derived from various public domain materials for a select list of utilities. Chief among the sources are news articles from *Utility Dive*, *Chartwell*, and *E-Source*.

Greg and his team also are active in the American Gas Association (AGA) and the Edison Electric Institute (EEI) trade organizations. And CS Week remains a must-attend venue, valued now more than ever with its recent consolidation with the AGA/EEI customer service meeting.

"We need to spend more time looking at other industries who are dealing with similar challenges regarding customer segmentation and in attracting and retaining the customer's interest during intense competition for the customer's attention," he said.

Celebrating Success

Celebrating success and achievement is particularly important in the utility industry, since a majority of customers are not calling to say hello or tell us what a great job we are doing. Rather, they most often are calling because they need us to address an issue.

So when major milestones are achieved or meaningful success has occurred with a customer interaction, Greg celebrates. When PSE&G ranked highest in the J.D. Power business surveys, he personally led the celebration.

Starting the celebration, a J.D. Power representative presented the awards at the quarterly leadership meeting. It continued via a road trip to various PSE&G locations throughout the state. Greg thanked employees for their contributions, talked about the importance of focusing on the customer experience, explained why PSE&G won the awards and described the key role each individual plays. Group pictures with the awards ended each session.

"Taking the time to recognize and celebrate success is a powerful motivator," Greg notes. "Employees become more invested in doing the best for our customers." If a customer service associate handles a tough call and ends up delighting the customer, the interaction is recorded by contact center supervisors and fellow frontline associates. Email alerts are then sent to all contact center associates. Alerts contain the representative's name(s) and a brief description of the compliment. Sharing these success stories reinforces the positive interaction that occurs every day.

Supervisors and contact center leadership follow up on each alert by thanking the representatives(s) personally. These compliments are summarized and shared monthly with senior leadership as part of a broader customer experience reporting package. Representatives with multiple compliments or a sustained track record of positive customer service are recognized with gift cards, additional breaks and company apparel, among other rewards.

DEVELOPING LEADERS

Greg describes himself as a servant leader who shares power and prioritizes the needs of others first. Servant leaders are driven to help people develop and perform as highly as possible. Servant leadership is an ancient philosophy found in many religious texts.

Greg lives this philosophy by always looking for ways to support his team, asking what they need and doing his best to provide the needed resources and support. "I never want this to be an environment that is top-down," he says. "That kind of approach prevents good thinking from smart people."

Greg's own career path has informed his approach to customers and leadership. Mentors have played a prominent role. Relying on proven management processes to ensure the team is connected and engaged, Greg is passionate about building a leadership team that models ownership and advocacy for the consumer. "We have an amazing team—the secret sauce to our success in serving customers well," he says.

> "We have an amazing team—the secret sauce to our success in serving customers well."
> —Greg Dunlap

Career Path

Greg started with PSE&G right out of college, graduating from the Rutgers University School of Engineering and the Silberman College of Business at Fairleigh Dickinson University. His career has spanned operations, public policy and customer service. Greg experienced utility deregulation firsthand and up close, a combination which has helped inform his passion and perspective on customer operations.

Beginning as a gas engineer in field operations, Greg gained a firsthand understanding of the processes, equipment and challenges a utility faces in delivering energy to consumers. "Field experience is critically important," he says. "The reality is that utility operations are unique. Utilities bring together the unusual aspects of large capital investments, a responsibility for public safety and intense scrutiny from every aspect of society including regulators, community leaders and customers. An operations background gives you the perspective of what is required from the men and women who keep the gas flowing and lights on every day."

Greg moved from operations to public policy during the 1990s, when energy markets around the country were deregulating. In hindsight, Greg notes that it seemed the utility industry transformed overnight. Working both at the federal level in the District of Columbia (DC) and at the state level in New Jersey's capital city of Trenton, Greg honed his advocacy skills as he worked with key stakeholders to ensure deregulation and customer choice were implemented in a sensible manner to all parties.

With his knowledge of the intent and goals of deregulation, Greg began educating customers about energy choice—his first foray into a role that required a customer-centric approach. Indeed, this role helped solidify Greg's passion that customers must be partners to achieve the goals around choice. Greg's experience then helps ensure PSE&G is delivering valued products and services today.

Greg further immersed himself in the customer side of the utility business when he joined PSE&G's customer order fulfillment group, which manages customer requests for new gas and electric service and key critical customer relationships. He then expanded his responsibilities by becoming the director of large customer support. This role involved economic development and managing relationships with PSE&G's largest customers including the builder/developer community. Greg also had responsibilities for utility marketing and communications. It was during this time, he believes, that PSE&G made significant strides in how customer service was being delivered.

Throughout his career at PSE&G, Greg has been actively involved in his community. That community includes his church, which eventually led him to attend seminary and be ordained as a Minister of the Word and Sacrament in the Reformed Church in America. Since 2005, Greg has served as the pastor at Woodcliff Community Reformed Church in North Bergen, NJ. He finds his greatest motivation to be a servant leader in the ministry and leadership style of Jesus Christ.

Mentors

Greg's dad, Charles Dunlap, was an early and ongoing mentor. "My father owned and operated a construction business in North Jersey," he says. "Watching him deal with customers helped me understand what it means to be totally accountable." The construction business also helped push Greg into engineering. In the public service arena, others who significantly impacted him were the late Jerry O'Connor, former Bergen County Freeholder and State Senator and the late Gerald "Gerry" Calabrese, NJ's longest-serving mayor. Both men served as mentors to Greg after he graduated from Rutgers and became politically active in Bergen County. At PSE&G, Greg says his mentors include La Rossa; Al Koeppe, former President of PSE&G; Forline, who led Customer Operations previously; and Kathleen Ellis, now Executive Vice President and COO at New Jersey Natural Gas. What Greg admired and tried to emulate from all his mentors was how to strike the right balance among professionalism, street-smarts and a passion for people.

Management Processes

Greg leads a large team of more than 1,300 employees, many of whom are represented by Local 601 of the Utility Workers Union of America, AFL-CIO. In addition to being PSE&G's customer advocate, Greg and his team ensure high quality delivery of the classic utility meter-to-cash functions. He is crystal clear with his leaders that it is their job to manage day-to-day operations and deliver on scorecard metrics.

Each led by a director, the teams are organized by function. The field operations team is the largest, with responsibilities for meter reading and collections. Greg also has directors over the billing, call center and new business functions, in addition to Esler, who works closely with him in managing the customer satisfaction analytics and customer experience process improvement initiatives.

"We have a close-knit team that talks daily, in addition to regular weekly and monthly meetings," Greg says. "The weekly briefings present an opportunity for the entire team to connect and discuss operational challenges happening in the moment. It also provides the chance for peer-to-peer discussion. The monthly meetings involve a more detailed review of the scorecard and initiatives. This meeting includes key business partners from information technology and human resources."

Like all of PSE&G, Greg's team manages via a scorecard with metrics for every aspect of the meter to-cash operation. Greg and his team review the scorecard monthly.

Being out of the office and in the field is a must. "I firmly believe that management by presence creates the opportunity to drive change and reinforce the right behaviors," he says. "I use these field visits to talk about our progress and thank our employees for their focus and attention to customers."

Talent Development

Talent development is equally important. Greg and his team use a combination of succession planning and performance management.

The succession planning process, led by PSE&G's human resources organization, is completed annually by Greg and his direct reports. This collaborative process provides critical discussion on each employee's growth and development. It identifies high potential employees who have both the aspiration and the capabilities to move to the next leadership level. For each high potential candidate, leaders identify realistic and achievable developmental goals, including job rotation or project team service.

Employing a software tool, PSE&G managers use a robust performance assessment process that includes clear, documented qualitative and quantitative standards. The process requires regular discussions on progress and areas of improvement.

As Greg looks to bring on new talent, there is a deliberate focus on diversity and inclusion. "Our customer base couldn't be more diverse," he says. "So it makes sense that we should strive for a workforce that reflects that diversity. We work closely with union leadership, employee resource groups and local agencies to attract folks from every segment of our service territory."

Greg is looking to enhance the candidate screening process to better assess whether candidates have customer-focus acumen. One proven and positive technique is recruitment in meter reading. As a temporary position, meter reading at PSE&G serves as a feeder pool to other Customer Operations roles. The temporary position allows managers to assess capabilities and customer focus.

DELIVERING CUSTOMER-FACING PRODUCTS AND SERVICES

Perhaps there is no better example of how listening to the customer can improve operations than how the PSE&G team turned around business customer satisfaction. A few years back, customer survey data provided by MSI noted that while PSE&G performed in the top quartile with residential customers, they were not scoring well with small business customers.

This required Greg and his team to look in the mirror. "We launched a comprehensive effort, first by listening to the voice of the customer via a series of meetings with small business men and women around the state," he recalls. "We heard from face-to-face conversations that small business customers felt they were being taken for granted."

The efforts netted a series of recommendations to enhance the small business customer's experiences, ranging from more dedicated call center support to proactive outreach and communication. Success was swift.

Dedicated Business Team

Fundamental in the transformation was the creation of a dedicated business team called the Business Solution Center. This team, made up of customer service representatives, was specially trained on commercial and industrial tariffs and issues business customers are likely to call about.

This team's mantra became one of resolving customer issues successfully and quickly. To that end, they have a well-defined escalation process that seeks resolution within 24 hours. This is how it works: If a call cannot be handled by the Business Solution Center, the call is 'warm transferred' to a business account associate. If the business account associate is unsuccessful, the issues are escalated to a managed account consultant who supports that customer area and will personally visit the customer's location within 24 hours. Greg admits there was initial concern about offering 24-hour response, but in fact it is rarely needed. A real ownership spirit drives the team to resolve customer issues without going to the final step of sending the consultant.

PSE&G ensured that business customers were informed of the new service via a modest promotional campaign, highlighting the tools and resources available for business customers to stay connected. This included promoting the Business Solution Center on the website and encouraging business customers to gain online access to programs, products and services. Business customers were encouraged to sign up for PSE&G's free, monthly e-newsletter for business, called *EnergE Link*. The newsletter is full of money-saving tools and information. Business customers can sign up to receive email updates during severe weather events and receive text and email notifications about power outages and bill or payment transactions. The campaign also promoted PSE&G's

mobile-friendly website. Standard promotional channels included bill inserts, bill messages, *EnergE Link* newsletter, social media, email, direct mail, and banner ads on various publications.

The small business campaign began in May 2014 and continued throughout the year. Business Electric and Business Gas customer satisfaction increased 34 points and 14 points, respectively, to the highest levels ever achieved. PSE&G won both J.D. Power Business Gas and Business Electric customer satisfaction awards in 2015.

PSE&G also launched a proactive outreach to business customers. They began offering monthly webinars on topics ranging from generator safety to how to read the bill. The webinars provided an opportunity to share conversations with customers on topics important to them.

PSE&G launched an energy efficiency program directed at the small business community via a direct install program. In this service, PSE&G audits the customer's business and identifies energy efficiency measures that would help the customer save energy. Additionally, PSE&G provides financing to support the energy efficiency enhancements.

The success was measureable. In addition to recognition by J.D. Power, MSI recently named PSE&G a customer champion for residential and business customers. Other indicators such as regulatory complaints and 'moment of truth' surveys also showed improvement.

WRAPPING IT ALL UP

Greg advises aspiring customer service leaders to master two important roles: the first, be a champion and cheerleader; the second, look into the mirror honestly to identify improvement opportunities.

"Leaders must champion important initiatives and celebrate success. Celebrate big and small victories. Be a champion for the customer when working internally with business partners or externally with key stakeholders. Celebrating victories is an important way to drive a more customer-focused culture," Greg counsels.

"Leaders must champion important initiatives and celebrate success."—Greg Dunlap

---

"Leaders cannot rest on their laurels. Rather, successful customer service leaders analyze service failures not to deflate people, but to look for opportunities to identify process improvements. Attempt to analyze," Greg continues, "how to take a poor customer experience and transform it for future customers by changing the process and experience."

As Greg looks into the future, he believes the big challenge lies in understanding and meeting the changing expectations of customers. "Increasingly, customers are not comparing utilities to other utilities, but rather to the best service providers out there," he says. "We know who they are, and we know that unless we meet those expectations, we are going to lose a tremendous advantage. Utilities already have strong relationships with our customers. We must cherish and nurture those partnerships so we can provide the services customers value, now and for years to come."

REFERENCES

1.   Dunlap, Gregory. Interviewed by Penni McLean-Conner, December 30, 2015 and follow up questionnaire, March 23, 2016.

2.   Public Service Electric & Gas Company History; https://www.pseg.com/family/history.jsp

3.   About PSEG; https://pseg.com/family/history.jsp and https://www.pseg.com/family/fast_facts.jsp; April 2016.

4.   Bergen, Jane and Swanson, Heidi. Interviewed by Penni McLean-Conner, May 3, 2016.

5.   Forline, Joe. Interviewed by Penni McLean-Conner, May 25, 2016.

6.   Nash, Bill. Interviewed by Penni McLean-Conner, June 20, 2016.

7.   PSEG Press Release, October 27, 2015. 'Sandy Three Years Later: PSE&G Achieve Progress Making NJ Energy Strong.' Brook Houston, media contact; https://www.pseg.com/info/media/newsreleases/2015/2015-10-27.jsp#v3kiKypViko

CHAPTER 5:
JOANNE FLETCHER,
BURBANK WATER AND POWER

Joanne Fletcher[1] has succeeded twice at a project most utility executives hope to avoid their entire careers, replacing a Customer Information System (CIS). In fact, she was so successful at both efforts that she and her team were awarded the CS Week Expanding Excellence Award for Best CIS Implementation in 2004 and most recently in 2014.

A practical leader, Joanne is always looking for and ready to take on the next opportunity that presents itself. She has learned that what people call 'good luck' is actually good planning and preparedness meeting opportunity. She credits Burbank Water and Power (BWP) General Manager Ron Davis for believing in her skills, challenging her with new roles and teaching her the importance of ensuring employee and organizational basics are in place to create an environment of trust, respect and excellence.

Joanne employs a realistic and pragmatic approach as she works with the entire BWP team to deliver quality customer service. With her strategic leadership, the organization has invested in complex modernization and technology projects that have enabled transformation of the traditional meter-to-cash processes, the way BWP evaluates system load, operations and the customer experience.

The word cloud (Fig. 5-1) describing Joanne includes a variety of interesting themes. It was based on interviews with her team and her

Fig. 5-1. Joanne Fletcher word cloud

boss, Ron Davis[2]. Interviews with her team[3] included: Sean Aquino, Customer Service Supervisor; Kathy Davis, Senior Clerk; Nancy Fadriquela, Senior Secretary; Joe Flores, Marketing Associate; Ozzie Hernandez, Information System Analyst; Tim Hou, Energy Services Manager; Teri Kaczmarek, Manager Customer Service Operations; Kapil Kulkarni, Marketing Associate; Jeanette Meyer, Marketing Manager; Charles Peck, Manager Customer Service Operations; Nancy Reis, Customer Service Supervisor; and Arineh

Sarkissian, Customer Service Supervisor. From these interviews, three characteristics stand out, revealing Joanne as a leader who is centered on the customer and who leads with qualities of responsibility, toughness and caring.

Joanne focuses on the customer. She empowers her supervisors and employees to respond to customers openly and with compassion. This requires employee training, trust and follow-up by the management team to ensure appropriate decisions are made. Supporting employees' decisions and helping them to intelligently engage in problem-solving with a customer goes a long way toward creating an organization that provides extraordinary customer service. Employees take responsibility for their jobs, their success and for productive outcomes. Joanne works with her team to ensure people, processes and technology are aligned to support this environment.

Ron Davis describes Joanne in one word, responsible. When asked what he meant, Ron clarified, "Joanne holds both herself and her team responsible." Ron adds, "No mission matters unless Joanne measures it. She uses metrics to monitor work performance and measures success against standards to improve operations. Without this attention to detail, it is impossible to have continuous improvement." Other words her team used that link to the theme of responsibility include accountability, businesslike, persistent and respectful. Kapil notes, "Joanne likes to keep it simple and to drill down into issues to gain a complete understanding." Teri further shares, "We have standards and we have to meet those standards."

Joanne has faced significant challenges that required a certain toughness to persevere. Ron told the story about BWP's investment in smart grid which tested Joanne's toughness. When this initiative started, he explained, "Smart grid was not well-understood." Since BWP is a municipality and everything is open to public comment, debate and pushback on the smart grid investment became very public. Ron acknowledges, "The pushback was tough, with public outbursts in meetings where Council Members would need to warn people to behave. Indeed, the entire BWP brand took a hit because of the visibility of the issue and the nature of the subject. But Joanne addressed this challenge head on. While not an engineer, she learned and understood the technical aspects of the smart grid. She effectively presented information to the Council and dealt with the public's negative comments with factual information delivered in a confident yet non-confrontational manner. Joanne calmly led the organization through this difficult time."

Joanne cares about employees and customers. The motto for BWP, 'Always there for you!' was developed by an employee committee led by Joanne. Her staff notes with pride that Joanne lives that motto for employees and customers. She is very concerned with what is happening with employees. Jeanette shares, "Joanne understands that we cannot provide good service if we are not providing that for ourselves. Joanne reminds us that everyone has bad days, and we all make mistakes. There is never any 'blame game,' just conversations about how to move forward productively."

Her team describes the significant investment that Joanne has put in place to ensure employees are able to excel and hence find meaning and value in their work. A big part is helping people understand the context in which they work and how what they do fits into achieving the entire organization's goals. This is accomplished, in part, by promoting training and cross-training and providing access to outside workshops and conferences for skill-building and networking. Another way is encouraging promotion within the Division by creating employee development plans and having clear career paths. This has fostered a very positive environment where employees have the opportunity to learn the 'big picture' about the industry and BWP, providing a holistic context for learning, working and decision-making.

Other words that describe this caring attitude are compassionate and empathetic. Her team notes Joanne's door is always open. She makes time for employees, dropping what she is doing and truly engaging with her team.

Finally, in addition to these themes around customer-centric, responsible, toughness, and caring, Joanne is an engaging and smart communicator and adds fun to the culture with a great sense of humor. She starts off every meeting with a laugh.

BURBANK WATER AND POWER

BWP is a 100-plus-year-old utility that serves 53,000 electric and water customers in a 17 square mile territory.[4] It is a community-owned utility that prides itself on providing reliable, affordable and sustainable services to the residents and businesses of Burbank. BWP staff appreciates they are directly accountable to the people whom they serve. In fact, almost everyone who works at BWP lives in or went to school in Burbank. It is a very close community, and staff is very responsive to customer concerns.

BWP is a progressive utility, one of the first in the nation to commit to having 33 percent of Burbank's power come from renewable energy sources by 2020 and one of a handful of municipal agencies that invested in advanced metering infrastructure to support the evolving electric and water businesses. Today, over 25 percent of Burbank's energy supply comes from clean, sustainable, renewable sources, and 15 percent of Burbank's water supply comes from recycled water. The utility collects interval data from all customers in preparation for advanced rate structures and operational improvements.

BWP is proud to provide reliable electric service that is consistently ranked amongst the highest in the nation. Additionally, their electric and water rates are both competitive and among the lowest in the region. BWP earned the coveted level of Platinum for the Reliable Public Power Provider award from the American Public Power Association (APPA). This RP_3 designation is given to utilities that provide their customers with the highest degree of reliable and safe electric service. Out of the nation's more than 2,000 public power utilities, just 82 have won the RP_3 designation.

BWP has always been ambitious. Burbank policy makers committed to investing in Hoover Dam back in the 1930s, which at the time was considered daring. With today's commitment to the Renewable Portfolio Standard and investments in smart grid, BWP continues that proud heritage.

BWP's General Manager Ron Davis believes, "Putting one step in front of the other and making one good decision after another, marching through time, creates a premier utility." He continues,

"A premier utility is one that delivers services customers can depend on, with affordable prices, while being good stewards of the environment."

CAREER PATH

Joanne is a leader consistently characterized as a hard worker, loyal and fun. She employs a practical approach to solving problems and addressing issues, ensuring both are handled in a reasoned, equitable and efficient manner.

Born from her confidence and self-reliance, Joanne's career includes themes of randomness and the ability to take advantage of opportunity. She clearly works hard and is not afraid to tackle new challenges. She has also maintained and leveraged a strong network of professional allies who have helped mold her career. To all her roles, Joanne brings her strong work ethic and her ability to quickly assimilate information and make decisions. These qualities, over her career, have been noticed, and doors have opened.

Joanne did not start out planning to join a utility. In fact, her plans were to complete a doctoral program in industrial/organizational psychology in Colorado. However, as Joanne balanced work and personal life, she decided to return to California to get married and opted for a master's degree in public administration (MPA) instead of a graduate degree in psychology.

Joanne enjoyed her role in public administration but found herself at an inflection point in her career. And, consistent with Joanne's career theme, a window opened. Joanne had met Bill Lewis, Deputy City Manager for the City of Pasadena as part of her MPA program and eventually landed a position as Principle Administrative Analyst for the City. After several years working for Bill, he retired to pursue a full-time consulting practice and asked Joanne to support him. Joanne jumped at the chance to take on a new challenge. In this role, she assisted with city manager/police chief workshops and executive team training, and she conducted organizational assessments. One of her assignments involved conducting an employee survey for Burbank Water and Power.

Joanne's work for BWP impressed then General Manager Ron Stassi. Another window opened, and she was hired to fill a newly created position at the utility, Administrative Officer. Because the position was brand new, Joanne had the opportunity to define and develop it. At the time, BWP reflected a very traditional utility philosophy. There were huge separations between the water and electric divisions and between the "suits" and field crews. Morale was low; service was suffering.

Joanne offered a unique addition to the mix. She recalls, "I began working at BWP when I was 30 years old. Not only was I relatively young, I was also the first female manager in a predominantly male environment. I was an anomaly. Creating healthy change in this environment was a challenge." Joanne noted that management books direct leaders in this situation to establish a mission and values statement for the organization. So she set about to do just that. Working through a team of employees later called the Team Building Committee, she developed a mission statement to provide a common context and purpose for all employees. In addition to the mission statement, the team documented BWP's core values for providing service and managing customer and peer interactions. Perhaps the most unique achievement at the time was the creation of a utility mascot, a Saint Bernard named Utility Bill, and a department motto. The qualities of a Saint Bernard mirrored those of BWP employees: helpful, strong and reliable. This was capped with, 'Always there for you!' a motto the team believed summed up their role and contribution to the community. These achievements showcase Joanne's creative side, which is an important part of her leadership style and one that plays out in her career.

"I began working at BWP when I was 30 years old,
… the first female manager, … I was an anomaly."
—Joanne Fletcher

Joanne recalls, "I was a 'Pollyanna' and very naïve." She came to understand that while the mission and values statement might have been proscribed in management books, when 'the rubber-hits-the-road,' they are merely window-dressing and do not sustainably improve service or morale in a dysfunctional organization where basic needs are not being met.

Fortunately for Joanne, another window was about to open. Because there were significant employee issues in the customer service area, Joanne was tasked with helping to resolve them. She demonstrated that she could be empathetic with employees and dissect complex issues.

One of the fallouts of that situation was that the manager who had been in charge of Customer Service and Marketing was asked to step down. Having seen Joanne in action, General Manager Ron Stassi asked her to take the leadership role and help rebuild the Division. Joanne notes, "I knew nothing about customer service, but I learned quickly." It was a time when bold leadership and change was needed. Joanne stepped up to the challenge.

"I knew nothing about customer service, but I learned quickly."—Joanne Fletcher

---

As Joanne grew in her new role leading Customer Service and Marketing, Ron Stassi retired and Ron Davis was announced as the new General Manager in 1999. Ron Davis has been credited with completely turning around BWP to the award-winning organization it is today, one known for high reliability, low rates and forward-thinking energy and water practices.

MENTORS

Joanne did not have mentors in a formal manner. However, she is thankful for time working with Ron Davis whom she describes as a great leader. "I have had the privilege to work alongside Ron, observe his approach and experience the results. He has been a wonderful coach and provided consistent support." Through Ron, Joanne learned that employees' basic needs had to be addressed for them to thrive and achieve excellence. To this end, Ron started at the bottom, handling what he called 'hygiene issues' and ensured employees were provided clean un-frayed uniforms, clean vehicles and clean offices. Then he moved to the issue of pay equity and completed a comprehensive compensation and benefit review with an eye toward market competitiveness and employee retention. This was an important lesson for Joanne in how to build trust within an organization. She explained, "You can't demand high morale, productivity and excellence. It must be fed, nurtured, and developed. Ron's approach did just that, and it was wonderful to be a part of the transformation."

Joanne also shared an example of Ron's collaborative, effective leadership approach that she now exercises. Joanne's team was receiving lousy service from one of the departments in City Hall. It was frustrating. She and her team wanted to confront the department head and demand change. Ron elected instead to 'soft ball' it. He asked her to keep records of the service level she was receiving. After many months, he quietly showed the department head the stats which spoke for themselves without damaging relationships. Joanne recalls, "While it is tempting to rant and rave, and this often feels good in the moment, Ron has shown me that there are better ways to handle things for a long-term productive relationship."

Joanne often takes the time to debrief activities with Ron to learn why he made certain decisions and the reasoning behind his approach. She is grateful for her time with Ron at BWP and notes, "I have had the wonderful opportunity to watch a brilliant person make extraordinary changes in an operation. That has changed me."

CUSTOMER SERVICE TEAM

Joanne entered the customer service arena in the 1990s following a complicated human resource problem that left the organization lacking focus and harboring mistrust between employees and teams in its wake. Additionally, BWP was a typical customer service organization at the time; it was positioned to 'fly under the radar.' Customers did not think about the Customer Service and Marketing Division. The primary focus instead was on billing accounts and collecting money. And, as is often the case, Joanne internally found, "Customer service was a low-level stepchild."

But utility restructuring was taking place, and it was causing BWP to examine its priorities and reevaluate how business was conducted. In this new environment, Joanne realized that she would need the team to embrace a new role, one that was more visible, sought excellence and accepted ownership for customer satisfaction and retention.

Joanne began making some changes. The Customer Service and Marketing Division she inherited had 39 frontline employees, all union-represented with a total of 16 different position titles. She developed a simpler organizational structure and created six position titles with broader job responsibilities. This enhanced career ladders and opportunity for employees while providing the organization with greater day-to-day flexibility to best meet current and future operational needs.

Additionally, Joanne introduced technology to the customer service organization. Initial enhancements included the implementation of automated call distribution, interactive voice response (IVR) and online service order systems. These allowed her team to move from the antiquated approach of cradling the phone between their ear and their shoulder and hand-writing service orders to full automation of the call and order-taking process. This was followed by migration of the CIS from a 30-year-old mainframe legacy system to an updated, distributed CIS, with electronic payments, paperless billing and a website. Subsequent technology changes and implementations included another CIS, wireless automated electric and water meter reading systems, a meter data management (MDM) system and a new improved website.

Joanne commented that one of the biggest challenges when making these changes was that some long time employees had trouble keeping up with the new ways of doing business. In some situations, this continues today as the Division ever evolves. She shares a practical view on this situation, "They haven't changed; we have changed." So, Joanne and her team work to leverage the skills and talents of all Division employees. Joanne believes that people excel in different areas, and it's best to optimize individuals' skill areas rather than frustrate productivity or insist employees do something they cannot. On the other hand, this philosophy only goes so far. "Ultimately," Joanne explains, "each employee must be able to perform the majority of their job duties and be held accountable to standards for completion of those tasks."

> "They haven't changed; we have changed."
> —Joanne Fletcher

CUSTOMER SERVICE ATTRIBUTES

Joanne looks for emotional maturity in employees and recognizes that it is easier to teach job tasks than it is to help someone develop emotional maturity. The ability to handle people, situations and frustration well are vital. Also important are good writing and presentation skills since these become requisites for moving up in the organization. So, one of the initial screening tests for potential customer service employees is a writing test in which candidates are asked to respond to basic and difficult customer service and interpersonal conflict scenarios. Once past this screening, Joanne and her supervisors complete interviews to select the final hires. Then, they use a one-year probationary period to fully evaluate new employees and ensure they possess the qualities needed for success.

CREATING A CUSTOMER-FOCUSED CULTURE

Joanne has been tremendously successful at transforming her team to a customer-centric, take-charge work group. This has been accomplished by being mission-focused, value-based and metric-driven. It requires helping people master their work environment through on-going training for skill development and information sharing about BWP and the business in general. It involves helping employees find meaning in their work by allowing them to make decisions, set goals and develop career paths. By setting goals and holding people accountable, Joanne finds, "People like being part of a high-functioning team providing meaningful service." By transforming the values and philosophy of the organization, she has also altered the employees' role and set the expectation that her team take ownership for customer issues. Indeed, when asked who owns the customer-focused culture, Joanne simply replies, "Every employee owns the culture."

"Every employee owns the culture."
—Joanne Fletcher

Mission/Values

Creating an organization able to focus on the customer starts with a mission, a unifying goal for interaction and service that empowers employees to be their best. According to Joanne, her Customer Service and Marketing Division's employees are "committed to exceeding customer expectations and nourishing a sustainable future for their community."

Joanne built this mission on a series of values. She realized a new tone was needed for the organization so employees might see themselves differently and move beyond prior challenges that had been in play. With her team, Joanne established the following values, still in place today:

- Provide extraordinary customer service by handling each customer with care and concern, building long-term relationships through helpful, courteous and professional behavior.

- Respect each other's differences and decisions.

- Use good judgment to balance the needs of our customers with the needs of the utility.

- Serve as the knowledgeable representative for all City departments providing municipal services and actively support our community.

- Continue our education and training to ensure we maintain the skills needed to meet our commitments and serve our customers.

Joanne believes that, to achieve success with this mission and values, it is important to engage the entire team and essential to push responsibility down as low as possible. She recalls, when she first took over the Division, processing an exception for a late payment required approvals up through three levels. The person in charge of the credit section was very 'old school' and anything out of the ordinary was brought to her attention for approval. She didn't share the underlying rules she followed and hence never allowed others the privilege or pleasure of understanding the context in which they were operating. This meant employees were never able to learn and make decisions on their own. This type of approach is not only inefficient; it is frustrating for employees and customers.

Recruitment and Succession

Joanne and her team have created and nurtured an environment that has become a compelling organization and one that attracts great talent. To ensure this trend continues, Joanne makes sure job descriptions and positions remain relevant. She then focuses on the recruitment and screening process to find people with the right qualities. With respect to job descriptions, Joanne established job families while reducing the number of individual job titles. In fact, she cut job titles by 50 percent and established career progression within the families. Additionally, she put into place a rotation of employees within job families to build comprehensive skill sets and maintain organizational efficiency. For example, customer service representatives gain exposure to the call center, then rotate to the billing, credit and service areas. She follows the same rotational protocol with supervisors.

A rigorous recruitment and selection process goes a long way toward securing good candidates. But the ultimate test of proper fit happens after someone is brought on board. Then the person must pass the probationary period. If any problems come to light during this time, Joanne believes it is best to end the relationship since this is the time when employees are trying to make positive impressions and do their best. Once employees pass probation and their performance does not meet expectations, removing them from the organization becomes a long and tedious task.

From a staffing perspective, Joanne is facing a challenge like many in the utility industry today: a leadership team that is mature and eligible for retirement in the not-so-distant future. She incurs an additional complexity since the union represents management positions. In fact, Joanne is the only non-represented person in the Customer Service and Marketing Division.

Joanne leads her customer service team through two Managers of Customer Service Operations. One manager, Charles Peck, handles Credit, Call Center and Payment Processing. The other manager, Teri Kaczmarek, oversees Field Services, Billing, Mail Center and Technology Support. Both have strong customer operations experience.

To build succession planning into her team, Joanne has created a new position, Assistant Manager Customer Service Operations. Asking her managers to mentor and develop these assistant managers, Joanne believes these positions and this tactic will help maintain quality employees and ensure a smooth leadership transition in the years to come.

Metrics

Joanne and the team monitor a variety of metrics to ensure continuous improvement, operational excellence and a great customer experience. Joanne has a reputation for being metrics driven, with Ron Davis sharing, "No mission matters unless Joanne measures it." Each transaction, no matter how small, builds upon the next. It's important to measure each one and then look at them holistically. To that end, Joanne and her team measure the components of providing a timely and accurate bill through metrics such as meter reads transmitted on time, missing data, data estimations, and number of adjustments required. Call center effectiveness is measured around service levels such as answer time, hold time, lost calls and first call resolution. Joanne uses first call resolution as a key measure of customer satisfaction, believing that customers appreciate having a question or concern addressed quickly and efficiently without having the call transferred to another resource. The goal for first call resolution is 100 percent. To accomplish this, representatives are informed, empowered and responsible for resolution. This provides a better customer experience and a healthier operating environment. This means customer service representatives must understand their role and the business, while exercising good judgment. Decisions are tracked and, if necessary, coaching is provided to ensure quality decisions are made for the business and the customer.

The team also has metrics associated with processing payments. Since BWP offers walk in service, Joanne's team monitors lobby transactions in addition to traditional mail and electronic transactions. The BWP website and an online presence are a big focus for BWP. To measure that channel's effective, her team monitors the number of customers who visit the website, enroll in auto-payment and take advantage of electronic billing, along with other services.

Joanne also reviews the participation and cumulative savings associated with various water and energy conservation programs offered by BWP. Particularly today, with California's critical water situation, the focus on engaging customers to install water-saving devices and fix water leaks is very high.

Customer Surveys

Joanne uses the services of RKS Marketing Research Company to conduct annual customer satisfaction surveys. Similar to services provided by J.D. Power, this survey focuses on municipalities and allows comparison among all California utilities. Phone and online surveys provide Joanne and the BWP team with important insights on how they are delivering service.

BWP also uses transactional surveys based on customers calling into BWP for service. The survey is mailed to every 10th customer handled by a call center representative. Today's customer satisfaction rating, 99 percent, is an enviable metric. Joanne and her team love the positive feedback, but they truly appreciate the occasional pointed comment that helps the organization grow.

Joanne, being ever practical, notes that the more immediate touch point with customers is with monitoring and managing complaints. When Joanne first took this role, complaints were common, and it was not unusual to have five to ten customers per month escalate through the customer service chain. With the transformation of both the organizational culture and the implementation of new technology to help representatives respond more specifically to customer issues based on that customer's actual situation, escalations have been virtually eliminated. General Manager Ron Davis notes, "Nowhere in my career have I ever served so many customers and received so few complaints."

> "Nowhere in my career have I ever served so many customers and received so few complaints."
> —Ron Davis

DELIVERING CUSTOMER-FACING SERVICES AND PRODUCTS

Joanne has clearly demonstrated a bias to updating customer service processes with current technology. Over the past decade, Joanne led the implementation of an automated call distribution system, an IVR system, electronic billing, a website, wireless water and electric meter reading systems, a CIS—twice in fact—and an MDM system. Joanne faced two key implementation challenges: avoiding scope creep and shunning the temptation to institute old practices into new systems. To address this, Joanne established a single, unwavering goal for each project and set a tone that BWP would take a fresh look at existing processes. This proved to be successful; Joanne and her team have received awards for two of their three large implementations. In addition, the team received eight regional, state, national and international awards for innovative customer programs and demonstration projects.

BWP's CIS story is instructive for utility leaders who are facing a similar decision. Joanne acknowledges, "The investments in automated meter reading and other smart grid technology combined with the investment in a web portal are important elements to BWP's engagement of customers."

Joanne may be the only utility customer service executive to have replaced not one, but two CIS systems for the same utility. She explains how this happened. In the late 1990s, BWP recognized that its 30-year-old legacy system would not be able to meet contemporary customer or operational demands. They evaluated many systems and chose one that was top tier at the time. The system implementation was done very well and, in fact, recognized by CS Week in 2004 for the most successful CIS implementation for a small utility.

That billing system worked well for a decade, but Joanne admits she did not perform regular system upgrades during that time. In addition, the once top-tier product had not been developed or commercially improved since BWP purchased it. As a result, by 2012, the system was outdated, and BWP needed to upgrade or install a different one to continue operating without significant risk. The evolving demands of the business such as time-varied rates and integration of renewable energy were also driving system replacement. So once again, Joanne and her team advertised and searched for a new CIS. They implemented a highly recognized system from a top tier company. Like before, with a single, unwavering goal and a focus on a fresh approach to processes, Joanne and her team implemented another new CIS, under budget and ahead of schedule, winning recognition from CS Week for Best Implementation of a CIS in the small utility category for the second time.

But new system components and capabilities did not stop with the replacement CIS. Additional investment in a MDM system was required to support the implementation of automated meter reading with interval data collection. The interval data from both water and electric meters was voluminous and required a robust database. Joanne notes, "It was helpful that the Power Supply Manager also needed a more robust meter database to collect and manage the distribution and system load."

WRAPPING UP WITH INSIGHTS

BWP's simple tagline, which Joanne originated, 'Always there for you!' tells the story of her approach to customers and employees. She combines a practical approach to customer service delivery with a creativity that keeps the BWP team and customers engaged. Joanne recognizes the importance of treating people with respect, maintaining community goodwill, making responsible and prudent decisions and continuing to learn and enhance one's skills and understanding of the business.

Joanne implemented two CIS systems successfully and manages a platform that will provide BWP customers with solid customer service delivery, both now and going forward. The CIS platform in place today supports the advanced metering infrastructure. It also supports data analytics that allow Joanne and her team to create more personalized service offerings for BWP customers and other BWP divisions to monitor their systems for optimized performance.

Joanne instills in her leadership team and employees the importance of accepting differences and respecting others. Joanne notes, "While our primary purpose is revenue protection on behalf of all our ratepayers, we must balance this with compassion for the individual while supporting the health of the Burbank community." Joanne understands this is not always easy, but ultimately she believes success will be determined by one's ability to make quality decisions, use good judgment and treat people well.

Joanne made some difficult decisions in building the BWP customer service team, not the least of which was uprooting the organization by consolidating positions, revising job descriptions and reducing field positions in anticipation of automation. Joanne advises up-and-coming leaders, "It is important to understand that you will never make everyone happy all the time. It is also important to be respectful of others. Explaining your decisions helps people understand where you are coming from, even if they don't agree." In hindsight, the move to consolidate the positions became an important foundation to rapidly advancing the BWP customer service team forward.

Joanne believes wisdom comes from making mistakes and learning from them. She encourages customer service leaders to learn about the utility business and build their skill sets in all areas of the revenue service cycle. She understands it is essential for leaders to take responsibility. Most importantly, Joanne notes, "Respect is critical - respect of others and respect for yourself."

"Respect is critical—respect of others and respect for yourself."—Joanne Fletcher

---

REFERENCES

1. Fletcher, Joanne. Interviewed by Penni McLean-Conner, October 16, 2015 and follow-up questionnaire October 26, 2015 and November 2, 2015.

2. Davis, Ron. Interviewed by Penni McLean-Conner, November 2, 2015.

3. Aquino, Sean; Davis, Kathy; Fadriquela, Nancy; Flores, Joe; Hernandez, Ozzie; Hou, Tim; Kaczmarek, Teri; Kulkarni, Kapil; Meyer, Jeanette; Peck, Charles; Reis, Nancy; and Sarkissian, Arineh. Interviewed by Penni McLean-Conner, November 19, 2015.

4. History of Burbank Water and Power, https://www.burbankwaterandpower.com/the-history-of-burbank-water-and-power. February 2016.

CHAPTER 6:
GREGORY (GREGG) KNIGHT,
CENTERPOINT ENERGY

As a high school student in Riverside, CA, Gregory (Gregg) Knight[1] drove himself to excel on the football field. Fighting exhaustion and working to continuously improve, he set his sights on playing for a top college team and then being drafted to compete in the National Football League.

A hard-earned football scholarship from the University of Colorado was a giant step toward achieving Gregg's ultimate goal, but the fortunes of the game turned against him. After suffering a knee injury as a first-string, redshirt freshman, Gregg faced the painful realization - he would never play professional football.

The sudden end of a long-held dream would leave many young men struggling to chart a new course for their lives. Gregg knew he needed to look inward and make some hard decisions. "I did not want to end up in a bar talking about my glory days," he confides. "I needed to translate the leadership and teamwork gained from my years in football into a professional career in another arena."

Although his football days were behind him, Gregg combined traits honed on the gridiron with his strong work ethic to forge a broad and successful career that has spanned several companies, roles and experiences. Now, as CenterPoint Energy's CCO, he continues to build on his success by leveraging technology and process engineering to create experiences that customers consistently rank highly. Indeed, CenterPoint Energy continues a long tradition of earning top utility honors in such national customer satisfaction ranking services as J.D. Power, the American Customer Satisfaction Index® and Cogent Reports™.

Gregg understands his customer base is changing, and the demands and expectations of millennials must be watched and met. He is investing in technology to deliver customer service to not only meet the needs of these younger customers but also enhance service to the entire customer base. His advocacy for industry-leading investments in advanced, big-data analytics to provide personalized, predictive service has become CenterPoint Energy's linchpin to achieving high customer satisfaction, especially among the all-important millennial segment. In fact, one of the customer satisfaction independent benchmarking studies referenced above identified CenterPoint Energy as Number 1 in customer satisfaction among millennials nationally when compared with other large US natural gas utilities.

This profile will explore how Gregg and his team deliver valued customer-facing products and services. Additionally, it will feature Gregg's unusual career path, how he develops his leadership team and his determination to infuse CenterPoint Energy with a customer-focused culture.

OVERVIEW

As Senior Vice President and CCO for CenterPoint Energy, Gregg Knight is responsible for customer services, energy solutions and sales, marketing communications, and marketing and strategy. Gregg's team includes: David Baker, Vice President of Customer Services; Johnny Blackwell, Director of Corporate Claims; Dan Dippon, Director of Products and Services Marketing and Strategy

Support; Troy Donovan, Market Development Manager for MyTrueCost.com; Debbie Korenek, Vice President of Energy Solutions and Sales; and David Quin, Director of Marketing Communications. This team[2, 3] provided another lens into Gregg as a person and a leader (Fig. 6-1).

Fig. 6-1. Gregg Knight word cloud

At the center of Gregg's word cloud is the customer and closely linked is the customer experience and vision. Colleagues who have worked with Gregg over the years have remarked about his vision for the customer experience, his strategic insight and his ability to create a customer-focused culture.

"Gregg has helped us think about the customer experience like we have not done in the past," offers Joe McGoldrick, CenterPoint Energy's Executive Vice President and President of the Gas Division.[4]

Quin says, "Gregg does an excellent job in articulating a vision and always connecting the vision to everything we do."

Korenek adds, "Gregg is one of those leaders who take you to the future. People want to go there."

In developing strategies, Gregg encourages listening to the voice of the customer (VoC). Blackwell notes that Gregg often says, "A customer's opinion of a company is not the advertisements they see and hear but a collection of experiences." He continues, "Gregg requires us to listen to our customers' needs, and then he strategically focuses our efforts to not only meet those needs, but exceed them."

"Gregg is one of those leaders who take you to the future. People want to go there."—Debbie Korenek

---

Donovan adds, "Gregg is deeply dedicated to creating the right customer experience for all points of interaction with the customer."

Another noteworthy aspect of Gregg's style, Blackwell says, is "He drives results while exhibiting humility and leading by example."

Those qualities reflect Gregg's understanding of the importance of teamwork, one of the values he carried with him from his football days. Quin notes, "A core strength is his ability to work collaboratively, sideways even, within the organization. He does whatever it takes to make sure other business leaders feel very connected to the work we do."

Donovan says he also appreciates Gregg's skill at being a consensus builder who works to get buy-in across his team and creates collaboration externally as well as internally.

Quin agrees, "He is a master at building relationships outside the company with key strategy partners. He creates a very seamless and collaborative process. He views third parties as partners, and he treats them as such."

Those who have worked with Gregg say his style of team development begins with challenging members to look at ideas in new ways. He then builds upon that by establishing a clear system of accountability and celebrating success.

"Gregg instills confidence in his folks," says McGoldrick. "He has attracted new talent. He has pushed the envelope to make sure folks are challenged."

Dippon agrees, "Gregg pushes for more. He wants to challenge everyone to do more." Indeed, Gregg has established challenge sessions, in which team members are encouraged to confront assumptions and take nothing for granted. These sessions are credited as a positive way to generate new ideas and solutions.

When Gregg speaks of accountability, he includes himself along with everyone else in his organization, insisting that decisions must be aligned with CenterPoint's corporate vision. Baker notes, "Gregg allows a lot of autonomy in decision-making and running the business. He has confidence in you and lets you take the ball and run with it."

Gregg's energy and personal skills serve him well in his dealings with people at all levels. "He interacts with everyone in the organization, from the CEO all the way down to frontline employees," Dippon comments. "He makes it a point always to recognize employees who go above and beyond."

Quin appreciates Gregg's insistence that his organization celebrate its successes. "We make a big deal to ensure everyone on the team feels the pride of the result," he says.

A key element in Gregg's success has been his ability to employ business process frameworks and build business cases for investments. Baker notes that Gregg guarantees the customer remains the focus at all stages of blueprinting the customer experience. A number of team members credit Gregg with bringing the Customer Vision Program (CVP) to life. The CVP gives CenterPoint a full view of each customer's unique profile, enabling the utility to anticipate and respond to the customer's needs more quickly and thoroughly. McGoldrick adds, "Gregg's Six Sigma experience and process knowledge were critical in implementing the CVP."

UTILITY OVERVIEW: CENTERPOINT ENERGY

CenterPoint Energy, headquartered in Houston, TX, is a domestic energy delivery company that includes electric transmission and distribution, natural gas distribution and energy service operations. Through its predecessor companies, CenterPoint Energy has roots tracing back more than 140 years to origins in Texas and Minnesota. In 1866, the Houston Gas Light Company was organized to supply gas made from oyster shells and coal for the street lights in what was then a coastal town in southeast Texas. Similarly, in 1870, the city of Minneapolis granted the newly formed Minneapolis Gas Light Company a franchise to provide gas service with gas manufactured from coal or oil at a plant along the Mississippi River.

A significant milestone in CenterPoint Energy's history came in 2002 with the restructuring of the electric market in Texas. Retail electric services and merchant power generation were spun off as Reliant Resources. Legacy power plants became part of a company called Texas Genco. The remaining mostly regulated electric distribution and natural gas energy delivery company adopted the name CenterPoint Energy to reflect its role in the center of the energy value chain and the center of customers' lives.

Today, CenterPoint pursues a corporate vision to "Lead the nation in delivering energy, service and value." The corporate strategy is to "operate, serve and grow" innovative, customer-focused energy-delivery businesses that provide superior performance. Highlighting the area of service, CenterPoint notes that its strategy is to "add value to energy delivery through superior customer service and new technology and innovation."[5]

Creating a Customer-Focused Cculture

The customer-focused culture at CenterPoint starts at the top with President and Chief Executive Officer (CEO), Scott M. Prochazka. The support and passion of the CEO and the executive leadership team are essential for sustaining a culture that makes customers' needs the top priority. A vital part of that support is the will to make needed investments for enhanced customer experience. In his commitment to achieving such a culture, Gregg has secured support and engagement for important technology investments to help his team not only respond more quickly to specific service requests but also analyze customers' unique data and anticipate their future needs. Gregg acknowledges technology is the enabler, but he emphasizes the processes that deliver the service and information to the customer rely on the integrated support of all areas of the utility.

Gregg believes it simply makes good business sense for his team to serve as the customers' advocates within CenterPoint. Just as the leader of the natural gas business is responsible for the safe, reliable delivery of gas, Gregg is responsible for the customer experience. Through CenterPoint's major capital investments in customer-focused technology like the intelligent grid and the CVP, the utility is more transparent and responsive in its interactions with customers. In addition to providing a higher level of customer satisfaction, these advances benefit CenterPoint's shareholders by accomplishing more at a lower cost. Gregg notes that customer satisfaction is positioned at an all-time high, even with contact center staffing reductions.

Gregg's mantra is every employee owns customer service. In the utility business, that means a focus on identifying flaws in the service delivery process and working to eliminate them. The flaws, easy to document, can be as simple as measuring the number of calls into the call center. In fact, Gregg refers to the call center as an 'exception management' team because it is the customer contact point for all exceptions created from other parts of the business. For example, he says, if there were no outages, there would be no outage phone calls.

Transforming the Customer Experience

Gregg maintains that his role's most important aspect is to define and articulate the business case for needed investments to transform the customer experience. Customers' expectations, changing rapidly, are shaped by their best experiences with other companies such as Google, Amazon and Zappos. This reality requires utilities to invest in technology and data analytics that provide customers the valued, personalized experiences they desire. Gregg has successfully helped senior executives understand the value in CenterPoint's journey to transform the customer experience and subsequently has secured needed funding to implement important customer technology advances.

Outside-In Perspective

To achieve customer experience transformation, CenterPoint has adopted an 'outside-in' perspective that provides an understanding of the effort required by customers to engage with the company. Gregg tells the story of waiting at a Houston airport a few years ago and receiving a text from Continental (now United) Airlines about a gate change.[6] "If Continental Airlines can proactively provide me with gate change information, can we do the same with outage information?" he wondered. Gregg and his team met with counterparts at the airline to learn about this transformation. By taking an 'outside-in' perspective, Gregg and his team gained insight about thinking innovatively around hidden opportunities to engage and delight customers.

"If Continental Airlines can proactively provide me with gate change information, can we do the same with outage information?"—Gregg Knight

---

In Continental's case, customer frustration with delayed flights, boarding gate changes and the check-in process had historically been accepted as status quo. But the airline looked at these experiences from the customers' perspective and placed a higher focus on their emotional impact. Continental identified the 'pain points' in the customers' journey, applying these findings to define process and technology changes. These changes transformed the customer experience, as when Gregg received the proactive gate change or delayed flight text.

Making It Easier for Customers

CenterPoint applied this 'outside-in' thinking to achieve one of the basic elements of customer satisfaction—reducing customer effort. This concept is detailed in *The Effortless Experience* by Matthew Dixon. This book references findings by the Customer Contact Council, which conducted a study of more than 75,000 people who had interacted over the phone or through self-service channels such as the web, voice prompts, chat and email. One key result finds that customers' satisfaction increases as the effort to complete a transaction decreases. Dixon notes that companies responsive to such VoC insights can improve service while reducing costs.[7]

This concept is intrinsic to the design of CenterPoint's service delivery. Indeed, the utility is one of only a handful of utilities adopting this metric. Prior to its focus on reducing customer effort, CenterPoint Energy's Customer Effort Score in 2013 was 3.57, based on a 1–5 scale, with 5 representing the least effort. After emphasizing the need to reduce customer effort, the 2015 year-end score rose to 4.56.

Gregg shared an example of a process that was enhanced by using the effort metric. 'Off by Worker' was a process whereby CenterPoint identified gas service that needed to be interrupted for preventive maintenance or safety concerns. Upon process review, it became apparent that while safety efforts were met, the approach left customers highly dissatisfied. In many cases, customers were overlooking door tags and may only have become aware of interrupted service when they tried to turn on their gas furnace or stove. This often resulted in multiple phone calls and high levels of frustration and dissatisfaction for customers.

CenterPoint created a cross-functional team to facilitate a process change that automated the 'Off by Worker' field code to trigger a notification to the company's escalation desk. Once notified, the escalation team placed proactive calls or sent emails to inform customers of the interruption and explain its purpose. The company also explained any city inspection requirements and worked with customers to coordinate the restart of service. Customer reaction shifted from angry to appreciative. A process that had received the company's most dissatisfied customer responses soon earned the highest satisfaction rating. Along with the customer benefit, employee pride grew and utility culture was enhanced by changing a negative customer experience into a quantifiably good one.

Voice of the Customer (VoC)

CenterPoint uses a combination of customer transaction surveys and focus groups to ensure the VoC informs its strategy. The utility refreshed its transaction surveys in 2012 to capture the customers' perception of the level of effort needed to obtain service or information. CenterPoint evaluates this important quality to enhance service transactions.

Gregg and his team use a variety of customer surveys administered in multiple channels. They include:

- In the-moment, post-call surveys offered via interactive voice response (IVR) to customers who choose self-service to complete transactions, as well as those who interact with contact center agents online or by phone
- Intercept surveys offered on complete and incomplete Web-based self-service transactions
- Surveys offered via email and phone for customers who received Power Alert Service notifications
- Email surveys offered to customers after interactions with Power Consultants and the Major Underground Group
- Email surveys offered to myTrueCost.com website users.
- Phone surveys conducted with customers engaged in the 'Off by Worker' process
- Post-restoration phone surveys offered to customers who experience an outage

In addition to the VoC transaction surveys, CenterPoint uses focus groups to determine improvements and validate system design during technology projects, such as implementation of the utility's natural language IVR system.

Engaged, Customer-Focused Team

One cornerstone of Gregg's success is found in his practice of surrounding himself with a talented, engaged team. His engagement approach includes setting expectations, holding regular meetings and celebrating success.

In response to his perception that utilities are often hierarchical in nature and decision-making, Gregg works to maintain a flat organization where candid input and innovative thinking are encouraged. He knows that such an integrated work environment can be sustained only if it is clearly his team's culture, not just an order handed down from the boss.

Setting Expectations

When Gregg joined CenterPoint Energy, he began establishing the culture he wanted for his organization by setting clear expectations. Foremost, he laid a foundation for the culture as one that values and engages employees. He brought an athletic spirit to leadership, coaching for success. He created an atmosphere of collaboration and collegial relationships. He also expected certain behaviors from his leadership team, including:

- Aligning their priorities with the company's corporate imperatives
- Understanding that communication doesn't fail; people do
- Remembering to trust, but verify
- Being transition leaders, not change managers

Regular and Inclusive Meetings

In addition to his practice of holding regular meetings, Gregg makes a point of including team members from multiple levels to help ensure work is coordinated across groups and a full range of perspectives is heard. His quarterly operations reviews, which look back over the previous 90 days and forward over the next 90, include both his direct reports and the next level of leadership. Gregg completes these reviews by functional area, encouraging leadership from all functional areas to join in.

Gregg believes that including the next level of leadership in these reviews helps safeguard that all levels are aligned with CenterPoint Energy's corporate objectives. The multidimensional participation by other areas promotes clarity about what each organization is working on and provides growth and exposure opportunities for more of his team.

Gregg also makes it a priority to meet with his direct reports monthly in one-on-one discussions to explore team progress in detail. This provides an opportunity to ensure alignment of key departmental business objectives and broader business, financial and corporate imperatives.

Celebrating Great Service

Another factor that Gregg views as critical for a vibrant organization is recognition of excellent work. He incorporates both spontaneous celebration and a planned recognition program to celebrate success.

Gregg has implemented a program in which employees can nominate anyone in the organization for a service excellence award. Honorees are selected by leadership and are recognized with a plaque, lunch with Gregg and the management team and a $500 gift card. As he expected, this recognition has nurtured employee engagement and spurred conversations about great service.

One recent winner is Carter Dedolf, a Senior Administrator of Energy Efficiency Programs in Minnesota. Carter was nominated for his outstanding work in acquiring additional customers. During his first few months with CenterPoint Energy, Carter took accountability for a 2015 goal of enrolling 1,000 customers for furnace or boiler tune-ups through the company's "Stay Safe, Stay

Warm" program, which provides free tune-ups to low-income customers. He worked with Community Action Program agencies, CenterPoint Energy's Home Service Plus® division and other partners to make sure as many customers as possible could benefit from the free service. His efforts resulted in a record high level of participation. Carter was recognized for his initiative and drive that brought a needed service to an important customer segment, along with positive attention to the CenterPoint Energy brand.

Developing Leaders

Gregg's own career path has experienced its share of twists and turns involving product sales and support, service delivery and entrepreneurial organizations—a personal journey that has informed his strategies for developing his team leaders. Because of the rapid pace of change, Gregg places great emphasis on transition leadership skill sets. He has introduced a disciplined process to assess and develop team talent.

Career Path

After realizing a pro football career was not in the cards, Gregg set his sights on building a professional career and secured his first job out of college at MCI (now Verizon), a telecommunications company where motivated employees could find many advancement opportunities. Gregg earned 11 promotions in eight years and gained a broad variety of experience, including customer service and regulatory advocacy.

Gregg's experience at MCI also introduced him to the importance of integrating technology into customer operations and developing the business case for capital investment. MCI was an innovator in call center operations and one of the first companies to implement computer telephony integration (CTI). The company used CTI to route calls to the most appropriate agents, a system common today but represented leading-edge technology in the early 1990s.

Given the task of developing the business case for using CTI, Gregg experienced firsthand the process of justifying a technology investment not widely used and then implementing it. Importantly, this demanding experience prepared Gregg for his current role at CenterPoint Energy.

Gregg faced a tough decision when MCI was acquired by WorldCom, whose culture was completely different. A new opportunity presented itself when a close friend was launching a business in men's apparel. Gregg chose to move to California and join him.

This entrepreneurship experience proved to be critical in Gregg's career development. Because an entrepreneur is responsible for every part of the business, from design to manufacturing to marketing and receivables, success requires a bottom-line focus. In contrast to a large corporation, where individual employees are responsible for a piece of the company's success, entrepreneurs own the business end-to-end. "If it is not successful, you do not eat," Gregg recalls.

After two years in men's apparel, Gregg became fascinated by the possibilities he saw in the changing electric market. He joined Reliant Energy and made the move to Texas. This offered the opportunity to learn a new industry while also leveraging some of his past telecommunications skill sets.

Gregg accepted a role in the call center, gaining firsthand experience in the competitive utility market. When Reliant decided to outsource call center operations, Gregg again faced a career move. He chose IKON Office Solutions, then the world's largest independent provider of document management systems and services. The company was bought by Ricoh in 2008.

Predominantly from General Electric (GE), IKON leadership brought the GE traits of innovation, leadership development and Six Sigma process discipline. Gregg recalls a key period in his development when he was responsible for directing a team of Six Sigma black belts – team members who devoted their time to project execution and special leadership for exceptional tasks.

From IKON, Gregg moved to CenterPoint Energy as the Division Vice President of Customer Service for gas and electric

Regulated Operations and Home Service Plus® (HSP). In this role, he managed the contact center operations, credit and collections, customer information system (CIS) administration, meter exception management and HSP contact center sales. Gregg was able to apply his coaching leadership style to great effect, implementing his team-building formula and delivering enhanced customer service. His leadership style began attracting attention, including a KITE Award in 2011 from Energy Central's *Intelligent Utility* magazine for his distinctive leadership in customer service. KITE Awards (Knowledge, Innovation, Technology and Excellence) recognize the outstanding accomplishments of electric utility chief information officers and leaders in customer service and operations. In 2014, Gregg was promoted to his current role as Senior Vice President and CCO.

Valuing the Role of Mentors

A student of leaders all of his life, Gregg studies traits that he seeks to incorporate into his own leadership style. Mentors have played a pivotal role in his career development. Early on, Gregg learned, "We don't see the world the way it is; we see the world the way we are." He values mentors for their ability to help broaden his perspective. Gregg makes it a point to seek out a varied set of mentors, diverse in gender, ethnicity and age. These mentors reflect all the people Gregg has worked for and with. They help him stay in touch with the realities and challenges faced by his team as they serve customers every day.

> "We don't see the world the way it is; we see the world the way we are."—Gregg Knight

As a student of leadership, Gregg discovered firsthand the ill effects of leading by fear. At MCI, he worked with a call center director who focused strictly on productivity metrics like call handle time, availability and after-call work time. The director maintained a list of those who fell short in these metrics, and the demoralizing list created an environment of fear and anxiety. From that experience, Gregg promised himself to do the opposite and instead keep lists on which his team members would be proud to be tracked.

Gregg has also made it a point to mentor others. He mentors inner-city students from Houston's Key Middle School in a program that helps them learn about business and the value of education. It provides students a support network to stay in school and to achieve in life.

Transition Leadership

Gregg recognizes that success in utility customer service delivery requires ongoing improvements in technology systems and delivery processes to meet rapidly changing customer expectations. But, he adds, "It is not enough today to just manage change." Rather, Gregg expects his team to function as transition leaders. Change management is reactive, while transition leadership is forward-looking. He challenges his leaders to embrace this perspective as a management function and approach change with a strategy, not just a business plan. "A strategy is about prioritizing appropriate activities," Gregg counsels, "and aligning them with the organization and business unit."

Developing Talent

His centerpiece to developing talent lies in a disciplined process to systematically assess employees on what they accomplish and how they accomplish it. To do this, Gregg uses a 9-block grid rating. Employees are slotted in a block based on their competencies being rated on the horizontal axis and their results being rated on the vertical axis. (Fig. 6-2). "From my perspective, a leader's success is based not only on what they did but how they did it," he says. "It is important to be strong in both."

Initially, Gregg recalled, the process was met with skepticism, but he now finds team members look forward to the conversation. It presents an opportunity to talk about all of the leaders

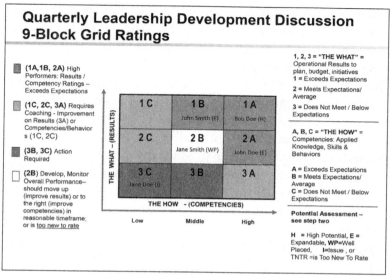

Fig. 6-2. CenterPoint Energy's Customer Operations 9-block grid ratings

and a methodology to validate or challenge assessment in a collegial manner. Additionally, Gregg and his team discuss employee strengths and developmental opportunities. He considers this conversation vital to ensuring the entire leadership team is engaged, motivated and growing professionally.

> "From my perspective, a leader's success is based not only on what they did, but how they did it... It is important to be strong in both."—Gregg Knight

Delivering Customer-Facing Products and Services

CenterPoint Energy has been successful in transforming the customer experience by leveraging the smart grid infrastructure and investments in technology to deliver excellent gas and electric service. Technology investments are also helping CenterPoint better market customer service.

Gregg and Gary Hayes, CenterPoint Energy's Chief Information Officer, have jointly sponsored the Customer Vision

Program, which brings together data from three separate CISs into a single customer relationship management (CRM) application. This provides disparate but related information from multiple applications, offering the ability to look at each customer's complete profile and resulting in one-stop service. It also offers customer preference management tools and customer usage data that support predictive analytics.

These analytics enable both call center agents and the utility's natural language IVR to predict why a customer is calling and provide a simpler, personalized experience. In addition to the new voice platform, CenterPoint has invested in mobile data and meter data management (MDM) systems. A new website was launched to interact with customers. This award-winning deployment results in a transformation in the customer's experience.

Call Center Week named CenterPoint Energy a 2015 Excellence Award winner in the category of "Best IT Team" for driving customer-centricity and technology innovation. This was especially gratifying to Gregg and his leadership team because one of their core principles in transforming the customer experience was to benchmark their success against not only other utilities but the full range of other industries such as banking and telecommunications. CenterPoint was recognized as a standout above other prominent companies, including a well-known financial services firm. One judge wrote, "Amazing use of the VoC (Voice of the Customer) program to drive the business. Extremely impressed with the effort toward desktop virtualization (and) top-notch customer engagement processes."[8]

Power Alert Service (PAS)

One shining example of these technologies at work is CenterPoint Energy's Power Alert Service®. PAS, a branded service, proactively alerts customers by phone, text or email when a power outage occurs at a customer's home or business and tells them when CenterPoint Energy expects power to be restored. The system first went online in 2013, and by early 2016 PAS had sent more than 7 million alerts to over 500,000 enrolled customers.

The results have been overwhelming. PAS has achieved a 90 percent customer satisfaction rating and sharply reduced call volume to the utility from customers reporting an outage or inquiring about a status for power restoration. That's significant because PAS frees up agent time to address emergency situations such as a live wire or pole down.

Chartwell recognized CenterPoint's achievement with a silver Best Practices Award for Outage Communications at its 2015 Customer Experience Conference.[9]

While technology innovations play an important part in this success, Gregg points to one other important element—the willingness of CenterPoint's different businesses to work together.

"We realized we aren't talking to a CenterPoint Energy gas customer or a CenterPoint Energy electric customer," Gregg says. "We are talking to a CenterPoint Energy customer. So we used our contact information from the gas side of our business to let people know about this important new electric service. Over 70 percent of our PAS-enrolled customers receive both gas and electric service from us."

The company continues to expand its PAS services. CenterPoint now sends alerts for both planned and unplanned electric outages. It is developing the ability to add multiple recipients for alerts to allow someone, for example, to know when an elderly parent is without power.

Natural Language IVR with Predictive Analytics

One of the first utilities to merge IVR and predictive analytics, CenterPoint Energy is transforming the customer experience. The power of this technology is best illustrated through example: Assume an electric outage. When a customer calls with a question, the phone system identifies the number calling, and CenterPoint's predictive analytics engine quickly determines that the customer is likely calling to report their power is out. As a result, CenterPoint's IVR greets the customer with a highly personalized and particularly relevant greeting, "Hi, Gregg, are you calling about your outage at (specific address)?"

The IVR will also suggest additional value-added services after meeting the customer's need. For example in an outage situation, the IVR will say, "I see you are not enrolled in our Power Alert Service. Would you like to enroll?"

Gregg notes, "Our new natural language IVR was intended to help us further accelerate our goal of improving customer satisfaction while delivering service at a lower cost." He recalls CenterPoint's legacy IVR was overrun with menu options, putting customers through numerous steps to achieve success. Fatigue led many customers to just press zero and speak with an agent.

Gregg says, "The natural language IVR is Customer Service's answer to Siri or Google." CenterPoint's predictive analytics engine and CTI middleware now predict why a customer might be calling across CenterPoint's gas, electric and appliance repair and sales business and can quickly lead customers to more relevant service options.

Historically, companies have measured IVR call containment, which identifies how many customer inquiries and transactions are completed without leaving the IVR. CenterPoint Energy is no exception. In addition to containment, CenterPoint measures authentication success and predictive intent accuracy as leading indicators to IVR containment. Authentication success tracks how successfully the IVR authenticates the customer account and identity. Predictive intent accuracy measures how well the IVR predicts the customer's reason for calling. Authentication is significant because time and motion studies revealed that agents were spending close to 30 seconds on calls authenticating and verifying customers. Today, the IVR automatically authenticates and successfully predicts intent.

The natural language IVR using predictive analytics is proving to be a game changer for CenterPoint. Customer satisfaction and effort scores have improved, and IVR containment rates now exceed 50 percent. In fact, Gregg points to this investment as a big reason why millennials in particular give the company industry-leading customer satisfaction scores.

Customer-Based Marketing

Just as the company has shifted its culture to emphasize 'outside-in' thinking and focuses on customer effort, Gregg recognizes the need for a similar culture shift to put customers and their needs at the center of the utility's product and service strategy. Gregg and his team have actively adopted IBM's 'Design Thinking' methodology, which emphasizes understanding customers' needs, desires and pain points and then designing outcomes to address them. Rather than first building something and then connecting to customers to figure out how to sell it, Gregg is reversing the script. CenterPoint will begin by connecting to customers, identifying what they need and then building it. He believes making this shift in thinking and culture is critical if the utility truly wants to become a trusted energy advisor for its customers.

WRAPPING UP WITH INSIGHTS

The next challenge for customer service leaders is developing compelling business cases for capital, competing with other important investment projects for precious funding dollars. As CenterPoint Energy has shown, well-designed customer service capital projects can make significant contributions to a company's bottom line, not to mention improve customer satisfaction and build brand equity.

Employee engagement is vital, both with the customer service team and the C-suite. It is important to demonstrate that capital investments drive customer satisfaction and these investments will be validated by customer satisfaction measuring tools. Customers experiencing the service transformation tell the story for CenterPoint, making the results even more powerful and successful.

Advice to Rising Customer Service Leaders

To those who aspire to leadership in utility customer operations, Gregg recommends, "Learn to differentiate between what is interesting and what is important." With every day bringing many interesting opportunities and challenges, he advises that one of the best ways to prioritize is evaluating items against corporate imperatives. "If there is not a strong alignment," he says, "it's likely the items are interesting, but not immediately important. Interesting items can be delegated, addressed at a later date or dismissed entirely."

"Learn to differentiate between what is interesting and what is important."—Gregg Knight

---

Gregg also advises that leaders must be able to articulate business value. How will an investment in a new technology, process or resource provide value to customers, shareholders and regulators? "And most importantly," Gregg cautions, "if you gain approval for the investment, hold yourself accountable for achieving business value, not just completing the project. This creates credibility and ensures future support for business initiatives."

Pinnacle of Success

Gregg is most proud of the fact that customers recognize the value of CenterPoint's investment in advanced technology. In this case, the combination of a natural language IVR with a predictive analytics engine and a preference management system has created a transformative customer experience. Customer research has shown that these systems have been especially satisfying for millennials —a growing and important bellwether in ensuring CenterPoint's Customer Service organization remains in touch with rapidly changing customer expectations.

REFERENCES

1. Knight, Gregg. Interviewed by Penni McLean-Conner, December 23, 2015.

2. Dippon, Dan; and Quin, David. Interviewed by Penni McLean-Conner, May 12, 2016.

3. Baker, David; Blackwell, Johnny; Donovan, Troy; and Korenek, Deborah. Interviewed by Penni McLean-Conner, April 13, 2016.

4. McGoldrick, Joe. Interviewed by Penni McLean-Conner, April 7, 2016.

5. CenterPoint Website; Company History; http://www.centerpointenergy.com/en-us/corporate/about-us/company-overview/company-history

6. Knight, Gregg. Questionnaire responses on December 30, 2015.

7. Dixon, Matthew; Toman, Nick; and Delisi, Rick; 'The Effortless Experience'; Penguin Group, NY, NY; Copyright: The Corporate Executive Board Company, 2013.

8. 2015 IQPC Call Center Week Excellence Award; https://www.callcenterweekawards.com/DynamicHtml.aspx?pageid=401774&eventid=1002279

9. 2015 Chartwell Best Practices silver award, Outage Communications; https://emacsconference.com/awards/#OC'15

CHAPTER 7:
MICHAEL (MIKE) LOWE, SALT RIVER PROJECT

This book on utility chief customer officers would not be complete without Michael (Mike) Lowe.[1,2] He is considered the expert on utility customer satisfaction. And the result demonstrates his success. With Mike's leadership at Salt River Project (SRP), a utility serving close to one million customers in Arizona, customer satisfaction has topped J.D. Power's utility index for 14 years.[3] Mike is well-respected in the industry for his customer service vision and his ability to execute this vision consistently.

His profile explores the mechanics behind the customer-focused culture at SRP. Rising customer service leaders will gain insights from Mike's career path and in his leadership development approaches. SRP under Mike's leadership has continued to offer innovative customer-facing products and services that are highly valued by customers.

MIKE LOWE OVERVIEW

Mike's team clearly recognizes why SRP has been so successful in delivering highly satisfying customer service. It is Mike's vision. And vision is at the center of Mike's word cloud (Fig. 7-1). Mike has worked with his team to establish a vision for the customer experience that has consistently guided the design of the customer experience. Successfully weaving this vision into the fabric of SRP requires focus on the customer experience. Mike models ownership and brings to the SRP team his determined and challenging nature.

Fig. 7-1. Mike Lowe word cloud

To gain another perspective on Mike, his staff was interviewed. Included in the interviews[4] were: Michael Mendonca, Senior Director of Revenue Cycle Services; Jim Pratt, Senior Director of Grid Modernization Services; Glen Traasdahl, Director of Customer Technology Services; Wayne Wisdom, Senior Director of Distribution Maintenance; and Cheryl Zittle, Senior Director of Water Services.

Vision

SRP's vision of being 'rewarding, easy and pleasant' is the keystone for its consistent success at delivering highly satisfying customer experiences. Michael notes, "We have had this vision delineated for 20 years: rewarding, easy and pleasant. We hold true to this vision. It has governed our creativity and driven our accountability and expectations." Wayne further points out, "Everything we do is measured against the vision, and we continually ask, 'Are we providing services that are rewarding, easy and pleasant?'"

Focus on Customer Experience

To deliver on the vision requires a clear focus. Glen notes, "Mike is very clear with priority, very focused and very decisive. He definitely knows the direction he wants to go." Jim shares, "With Mike, all the discussions in our company have a customer focus." And the customer focus extends to the hiring process. Jim reveals, "We hire customer-focused employees. The customer experience is discussed in EVERY conversation. We have these conversations consistently."

Challenging and Determined

Mike has a challenging and determined nature. Glen comments, "Mike challenges the way things have always been. He projects an insatiable curiosity and is always scanning the industry and beyond for the best customer experience."

An example that highlights both Mike's challenging and determined nature is the implementation of pre-pay. SRP was the first US utility to implement pre-pay for customers in the 1990s. Implementation of this system required business process changes, fundamental modifications to how information technology systems operated, customer education and communications.

"He projects an insatiable curiosity and is always scanning the industry and beyond for the best customer experience."—Glen Traasdahl

In fact, not everyone supported pre-pay. Mike's staff gave insight that there were doubters, both internal detractors and external opponents. But Glen shares, "Mike was tenacious in supporting this initiative when he had so many detractors." Today, his staff simply call Mike a pre-pay pioneer, a sentiment shared by many in the utility industry.

Ownership

Mike models ownership and accountability. He and the team set goals, and he holds everyone accountable to reach them, including himself. Because metrics are core to successful management of achieving goals and initiatives, the team parrots one of Mike's adages, "You cannot manage what you cannot measure."

Included in accountability is not only providing customers with easy, pleasant and rewarding service, but also continually reducing costs. One of the ways Mike and the team take cost out of the business is via technology, something Mike embraces. He sees the advantages that technology can bring to the business. Embracing technology may be the secret sauce to how Mike and his team successfully deliver high satisfaction while always lowering costs. Cheryl notes, "He keeps the costs per customer down. Mike has implemented all of these advancements while maintaining or reducing the cost per customer. He has utilized efficiencies while creating value for customers."

SALT RIVER PROJECT OVERVIEW

SRP is the oldest multipurpose federal reclamation project in the United States and has been serving central Arizona since 1903. It is also one of the US's largest public power utilities. Their service territory spans 2,900 square miles, serving three counties including most of the Phoenix area. An integrated utility, SRP provides generation, transmission and distribution services as well as metering and billing services.

SRP also supplies raw water supplies to Arizona, delivering water to a 375 square mile service area while managing 13,000 square miles of watershed that includes an extensive system of reservoirs, wells, canals and irrigation laterals.[5]

Indeed, it was water that first formed SRP in 1903. In order to obtain funding through the National Reclamation Act, ranchers and farmers in the Salt River Valley banded together to form the Salt River Valley Water Users' Association. This group pledged their land as collateral to repay federal loans to build a dam at a site in the Tonto Basin, a narrow canyon situated 80 miles northeast of Phoenix. This site was determined to be an ideal location to store winter snow and rain runoff from the mountains above the Salt River. This water storage was critically needed to offset periods of droughts that the Salt River Valley had experienced over time.

The Theodore Roosevelt Dam was dedicated in 1911, and it became prominent not only for water management but for hydroelectric power to support the growing mining industry in Arizona. Over time, SRP built more dams and added to the hydroelectric fleet. SRP partnered with other utilities to develop a regional power system that included power plants and many miles of transmission.

The Valley was growing quickly during the 1970s, and SRP continued to add to the generation fleet with fossil-fueled plants including three generating stations on the Navajo Indian Reservation. Today, SRP provides a generating mix of hydro, fossil and renewable energy resources, including wind, geothermal, solar and landfill gas.[6]

CREATING A CUSTOMER-FOCUSED CULTURE

The customer focus starts from the top at SRP. The vision statement is comprehensive. The culture is further defined by the vision. And the vision expresses the customers' experience by further defining how this service is delivered, describing employee attributes to make this happen. SRP builds upon this vision by organizing for success. Regular communication and feedback loops ensure alignment to the vision. The voice of the customer (VoC) is prominent in all aspects of SRP's efforts. Like all successful organizations, SRP measures performance and celebrates success.

Passion from the Top

From the top down, there is corporate ownership for customer satisfaction. The chief executive officer, Mark Bonsall provides unfailing support for actions to improve customer satisfaction. He is always open to doing things better, faster or cheaper. Importantly, he is a change agent and encourages and rewards meaningful change. In his role as the chief customer executive, Mike defines the strategies that will move SRP forward. Importantly, Mike notes, "Ownership for the customer is a shared responsibility, and customer satisfaction performance is tied to compensation for all employees."

The SRP board of directors is also actively engaged and interested in satisfying customers. Elected by land owners in the service territory, the board fundamentally creates ownership and accountability. It reviews monthly performance and service provided to customers in a report prepared by Mike. And importantly, the board has a hotline, a direct line to Mike and his team for any issues they want addressed. While rarely used, when the hotline rings, Mike and his team ensure a quality and expedient resolution.

Customer Service Vision

Daily, Mike and his team use their vision statement to scrub their actions and initiatives. Interestingly, the vision which was developed almost 20 years ago has proven durable with only minor modifications necessitated by significant expansion of group responsibilities.

Customer Operations & Services

Mission
We will extend our industry lead in customer satisfaction and loyalty.

Vision
Customers find doing business with us to be rewarding, easy, and pleasant. Innovative and cost-effective services inform our customers, enhance their convenience, and help them to conserve money and resources. We build durable relationships by addressing the unique needs of our customers. Our tightly integrated operations provide reliable delivery of water and power and consistently accurate and timely service.

Our employees are educated, willing, and friendly. They possess the knowledge, skills, and abilities to provide superior service with utmost regard for safety for all. We provide employees with targeted training and development opportunities, and we reward them with challenging work, recognition, and a safe, pleasant, and fun work environment. We are developing the next generation of leaders within Customer Operations & Services.

Fig. 7-2. Salt River Project Vision Statement

To create the vision, Mike first crafted the essential elements and then sought review and comment from his direct reports, first individually and then collectively. Today, the vision statement (Fig. 7.2) is prominently displayed on large posted boards in meeting rooms throughout SRP, serving as a beacon to guide all employees in the customer service group.

"It is not easy to make it easy."—Mike Lowe

In fact, the three words, rewarding, easy and pleasant, form the threshold for any customer service interaction or new service offering. Mike notes, "If you went around and asked employees in his group, you would hear these three words parroted." Mike and his team screen their actions against this vision. They listen and review customer experiences in detail including counting number of clicks on a mobile device or computer a customer would have to take to complete a transaction and ask themselves: 'Is this really rewarding, easy and pleasant?' Mike cautions, "It is not easy to make it easy."

But the vision goes beyond just defining the customer experience. It also describes the tightly integrated organizational delivery that SRP will provide. Further, this vision identifies what employees will bring to SRP and what SRP will provide in return.

Organized to Deliver Superior Service

The organizational structure helps everyone focus on the customer. At SRP, the organization is process-based to ensure efficient service delivery. In fact, Mike has responsibilities for distribution operations and maintenance, water delivery, customer service and associated information and operational technologies. He oversees a staff of 2,000 employees.

Mike manages five direct reports. A senior director of distribution operations and maintenance is responsible for the construction, operation and maintenance of the distribution system below the substations. A senior director of water customer service oversees construction, operation and maintenance of irrigation works, water delivery and associated billing, accounting and customer service. Third, a senior director of revenue cycle services manages new customer construction, metering, billing, revenue accounting and collections. A senior director for customer experience services is responsible for key account management, mid-size accounts, phone centers, training, experience management and emerging programs. Lastly, the director of technology services, functioning as a satellite information technology (IT), provides support for customer systems and works closely with corporate IT.

The vision statement talks about tightly integrated operations. This driver impacted the most recent organizational alignment which placed the water and power call centers into Mike's organization, a move that achieved economies of scale and consistency.

Mike acknowledges that SRP has work to do in enhancing the new customer connection experience. Recently, he realigned resources to provide a dedicated team to manage the entire new connection life cycle. The team not only handles the initial customer intake, but they also design, engineer and construct the services. This alignment of resources ensures that new services are implemented in a cost-effective and customer-focused manner.

Communication and Feedback

To ensure the organization stays aligned with the vision, Mike has installed important management, communication and feedback processes via a set of regular meetings:

- Staff meetings which include systems and process governance
- Strategic planning sessions
- Meetings with frontline employees

Mike believes these meetings are fundamental to ensuring customer strategy initiatives are moving forward and the day-to-day business of customer service customer stays on track. With over 20 years in the customer function, Mike has reached some important realizations:

- The customer function is incredibly complex. Mike notes half-jokingly, "Utility billing is more complicated than rocket science."

- In their quest to perform well, employees will seek ways to execute their tasks better, faster or at a lower cost. When they can, employees will implement changes on their own, often without the full view of downstream impacts occurring elsewhere in the organization.

- Information technology is essential to customer service. "IT isn't a nice-to-have; it is a must-have. Technology can manage you and dictate your processes and procedures or you can manage technology."

Staff meetings. The heart and soul of operational performance is managed via weekly staff meetings. These Monday meetings last three to five hours. Administrative matters and general updates are addressed, with the bulk of the time devoted to VoC and process governance.

The VoC is actively listened to and used at SRP. At their weekly meetings, staff extensively reviews and discusses customer research and potential responses to issues identified with the research. These include development of new business processes and new technologies or the conceptualizing of substantive changes to existing processes or systems that may be needed or desired.

Regarding process governance, the management team tightly oversees business processes and technologies. Often, the entire group will participate in and review the end-to-end flow of a business process map. Changes to either technology or process must be reviewed and approved by the management team. In addition to Mike's direct reports, the CEO and other members of his staff participate in this business process and governance portion of the meeting which also features presentations from project managers, system sponsors and associated professionals.

Strategic planning. Mike acknowledges that, when heads are down continuously dealing with customer, employee, process and system issues, it is easy to lose focus on the big picture. To compensate, Mike takes time to step back and bounce ideas off his staff or 'confab' in strategic sessions.

To do this, Mike and his team go offsite two times a year. This regular offsite time started with long breakfast meetings and moved to an offsite venue. For the first offsite meeting, the team opted to journey by the Amtrak Coast Starlight from Los Angeles to Portland. During this 34-hour journey, they spent time in extended planning discussions. Mike fondly recalls passing morning and afternoon hours on the train debating and strategizing, and the team shared every meal together in the parlor car.

Today, these offsite meetings often convene at Mike's cabin in the mountains of Arizona for a day and a half. In the summer, the cabin offers a cool respite from the Phoenix heat. But in the winter, it is bitterly cold. The sessions often involve pre-reading and cover many topics, for example, a deep dive into the internet of things (IoT). The team continues the tradition of sharing meals, working together to prepare them. This quality time for Mike and his team is a key ingredient in the secret sauce SRP uses to stay relevant to its customers.

Meetings with frontline employees. With over 2,000 employees, Mike believes it is important to meet face-to-face with frontline employees to better understand their work experiences and to bypass the filtering of information that necessarily occurs with intervening levels of management. Mike wants to know firsthand if employees have the tools and information they need to do their jobs appropriately. He wants to discern if they are supported by their management. He wants to understand what business processes and procedures are working for them and which ones are not. Mike gains this understanding through a combination of visiting field crews, gathering with the Issue Team and meeting with union leadership.

Mike visits field employees monthly on their turf. Almost half of the 2,000 employees for both water and power functions, field, shop and clerical, are represented by the International Brotherhood of Electrical Workers, Local 266.

Mike has invested in establishing a strong and positive relationship with the union. Building this relationship has supported an environment of mutual respect and a focus on win-win opportunities. While the volume of grievances, one important indicator of the union-management relationship, ebbs and flows, Mike says the overall volume is lower today than a number of years ago.

Mike uses the example of smart meters deployment in 2006 as one to show the mutual positive relationship between management and the union. Mike and his team knew the wide-scale deployment of smart meters would result in the elimination of meter reading positions. Then, SRP had 93 meter readers; today, there are zero. However, Mike and his staff made the conscious decision to utilize existing SRP employees to install meters. They made overtures with the union business manager, reached agreement on the classification of employees who would do the installation and offered training to qualify all meter readers for that classification. They further agreed to provide skills training, such as for commercial driver's license (CDL) and forklift operations, to enable these employees a competitive opportunity for other positions at SRP or elsewhere. They worked with the human resource team to actively place impacted employees internally or externally. The union management and Mike's team collectively met with meter readers to explain the efforts and encourage them to seek various training opportunities. Labor issues in metering and meter reading functions were consequently minimized throughout the meter readying effort.

The Issues Team was formed in 2012 shortly after water operations and the power group were added to Mike's team. The 13-member Issues Team was created because Mike observed each area had a very separate and distinct culture with both positive and negative attributes. The Issues Team was one tool Mike used to stand up a new, consolidated culture.

The Issues Team, comprised of hourly and salaried employees, are selected by their management team to serve two-year terms. Managers look for good communicators and those who are committed to their jobs.

This diverse group meets each month. Mike hosts them for lunch, and the agenda includes presentations that provide the Team with insight on other areas of the company or company issues. Mike will always end these sessions with a question and answer session. Not only does Mike learn from the team, but this forum provides an opportunity for employees to learn about SRP from each other.

VoC

Mike passionately says, "You cannot do customer service without listening to the customer." SRP has been surveying customers since 1991, well before J.D. Power entered this space. In 2001, SRP ranked at the top of the first J.D. Power electric utility customer satisfaction survey. Mike notes that at the time SRP did not even know J.D. Power was in the marketplace.

As SRP dug into those surveys, they found remarkable similarities and correlations with SRP-sponsored surveys. SRP uses a very robust quarterly and bi-monthly survey process. The surveys have expanded over the years to include transactional surveys of customers who have experienced service via the web or phone center. The surveys are administered predominately via the web, but phone surveys are also completed. In fact, after an inbound customer service call, customers are solicited to participate in a survey at the conclusion of the call.

"You cannot do customer service without listening to the customer."—Mike Lowe

---

In addition to using the survey data to inform strategy and business processes, the surveys act as radar for poor service. Mike has implemented a recovery team. If a customer gives SRP a poor score on the phone survey, the recovery team listens to the interaction. They will work to resolve concerns and issues with the customer in a positive manner, while also identifying whether or not a process failure happened. Survey results are provided as feedback to individual customer service representatives. SRP has found the process of surveying customers via the IVR post the inbound call to be extremely helpful.

Metrics

On a monthly basis, Mike and his team review over 300 metrics that provide information from call center performance to cycle time for a new customer hook up, among others. In line with performance-based organizations, metrics are tiered, so deep dives into the drivers behind the performance of a particular top tier metric can be analyzed.

A team of analysts pull in the metrics' data and build a master metric performance spreadsheet. Each senior director will provide a brief synopsis and report on organizational performance. At the monthly team meeting, the senior directors will summarize their top two to four stats. For example, on pre-pay, metrics are reported for number of transactions, number of payments at pay centers, total dollar volume, equipment availability and service calls on equipment. If SRP starts to show a negative trend, the metrics support drilling down into the issues. SRP will make policy, process and system change as a result of these statistics.

Mike shared the example of when SRP noticed an increasing trend in equipment failures at pay centers. SRP investigated and determined that half of the downtime was due to problems with receipt printing. The pay station was either running out of paper or experiencing paper jams. So SRP began offering to email receipts. The result was a tremendous reduction in machine failure, translating into labor savings and customer satisfaction because pay station machines were more available.

Celebrating Success

SRP celebrates success in delivering great service to customers. Special recognition for jobs well-done result in a monetary award up to $750. Employees have been recognized for excellence when working with external customers, and internal contributions like addressing power reliability issues or preventing business disconnections by proactive outreach and full account review are also celebration-worthy. Employees are recognized for creating process improvements that drive efficiency and reduce errors.

Success stories are shared weekly in an employee newsletter called *The Pulse*. This newsletter highlights opportunities to talk about service to the customer and employee accomplishments. It provides progress on SRP's corporate initiatives and features a lot of employee pictures and stories. Because SRP highly values being an integral part of the local community and emphasizes giving back to the community, *The Pulse* showcases various volunteer events. Safety, another important employee program, is a consistent theme in the newsletter, along with an updates on corporate measures. And the newsletter recognizes employee retirements.

DEVELOPING LEADERS

The commitment to developing leaders reflects the vision statement, 'We are developing the next generation of leaders within Water & Power Customer Services.' Mike's own career path provided him with a firm understanding of the economics of the utility industry. SRP leverages mentoring as a developmental tool, and Mike himself has benefitted from a mentor throughout his career. Mike has implemented processes to engage his team and support their development.

Career Path

With over 35 years' experience with SRP, Mike is a seasoned veteran. His experience spans roles in pricing, finance and information systems. Mike feels that the finance experience was critically important in his career to understand the economics of the utility industry along with his growth and learnings over time heading up customer service operations. Throughout Mike's career, information technology has also been an important skills element.

Mike holds a BA in economics from California State University, Stanislaus and a master's in business administration from Arizona State University. Immediately after college, he worked for the E. & J. Gallo Winery in Modesto, CA, as a production planning analyst. In this role, Mike was very involved in information technology because he was required to help coordinate crop forecasts, production expectations and sales forecasts. Effectively, Mike worked in a satellite IT function and developed a materials requirements planning system that ran on a Digital Equipment Corporation PDP 11-70, a very early form of distributed computing.

In 1979, he moved to Salt River Project in the finance function. During his 12 years in this area, Mike worked in various roles including rates, treasury and accounting. This experience again tapped into Mike's IT skills. He completed computer-based statistical analysis and modeling using tools that end-users could access on SRP's mainframe. Mike ultimately stood up a suite of end-user developed programs to manage the cash management and bond accounting functions. This led to Mike being asked to lead software development and maintenance functions in corporate IT for over two years.

In the mid-1990s, Mike moved to customer service operations. There, Mike combined his keen understanding of the business, his expertise in technology and his passion for the customer.

Over time in customer service operations, Mike's responsibilities expanded to include frontline service, back office, billing and field work, and more recently all of the distribution and delivery functions for power and water.

Mentors

Mike offers high praise for his manager, Mark Bonsall, SRP's Chief Executive Officer for whom Mike has worked for over 35 years. Mike shares, "Mark is always two steps ahead," which challenges Mike to look beyond the status quo. Importantly, Mike notes that whenever he makes the case for an initiative, Mark is right there with the checkbook.

Mike also has an external mentor, one he secured after discussions with the human resource department about challenges he faced in talking and communicating with one of his managers. Mike, a naturally analytical individual, found this mentoring experience helped him not only appreciate the diversity of thoughts, but it offered constructive ways to encourage and support good, thoughtful conversation.

Mike found the support of this outsider to be very helpful, and he has continued this investment on his own. His mentor, a woman who was a senior executive in a Fortune 500 company, has helped Mike explore areas of interest and importance and to address issues head-on.

Engaging His Team

To 'develop the next generation of leaders', another part of the SRP vision, Mike engages his team in significant leadership development opportunities. These opportunities provide hands-on experience, along with networking and educational experiences.

'We are developing the next generation of leaders within Water & Power Customer Services.' —SRP Vision Statement

---

Another important leadership development opportunity is the expanded management team meetings held twice a year. At these meetings, Mike establishes and clarifies direction, while demonstrating to employees that he cares and wants to get to know the team personally. Vice versa, and most essentially, Mike finds out what is on the minds of leadership.

Mike has created hands-on development by assigning sponsor roles for enterprise strategic initiatives to his direct reports. These initiatives are framed at the off-site meetings. Mike works directly with each leader on their initiative, and the leader is heavily involved in the group, via the weekly governance meetings.

Hands-on development for key talent in the organization is also thoughtfully planned. Mike and his team spend time discussing their key talent and ensuring developmental plans are enacted that build leadership and customer operations skills. Key talent developmental plans may include involvement on strategic initiatives or actual job rotations.

Mike encourages his team to get involved in events both inside the industry, such as CS Week, and outside. Mike models this involvement by his personal engagement in industry events like Electric Power Research Institute (EPRI), Marketing Executive Council, and CS Week, along with cross industry events.

SRP's success with delivering a highly satisfying utility experience is well-recognized. The mission Mike developed so many years ago continues to drive the focus and effort for SRP. As he looks forward, Mike understands customers' expectations will continue to change and customers increasingly want their unique needs addressed.

DELIVERING CUSTOMER-FACING PRODUCTS AND SERVICES

Considering Mike's finance and rate background, it is not surprising that some of the services he is most proud to offer customers involve pricing options. In fact, SRP leads the nation in innovation with pricing products as the first utility to offer pre-payment. With time-of-use data, SRP recently introduced a version of time-of-use that appeals to customers wanting to leverage time-based rates with a simpler approach. These innovative pricing structures are further facilitated by SRP's investment in a smart meter platform.

Pre-Pay

SRP offered pre-pay initially in 1993 as a pilot program to 100 customers. Today over 150,000 customers or about 17 percent select pre-pay as their preferred pricing plan. Customers on pre-pay are heavily engaged and highly satisfied. SRP has found that pre-pay customers call less than those not on pre-pay.

Mike notes that while initial adoption was slow, pre-pay started to ramp up exponentially in the 2008 and 2009 timeframe, coincidental with the US recession. Many customers who choose pre-pay do so because it helps them manage their bills. Mike recalls chatting in the business office with one of the first customers on the pilot program. She said, "I won't ever let you take this program away from me." Customers on this program continue to be passionate about it.

> "I won't ever let you take this program away from me."
> —Pre-pay customer

Customers on pre-pay buy power very frequently. During SRP's peak summer season, customers will average buying power two times a week. Today, pre-pay customers have a smart card and can visit one of 75 service territory locations to turn on power via check or cash at a payment kiosk. Typically, customers buy increments of $20 - $25 dollars on Friday nights after payday. SRP has found that customers on tight budgets might be able to afford $25 per week, but cannot afford $100 per month. SRP even had one customer who bought $1 per day by collecting and recycling aluminum cans to keep his family in power.

With frequent purchases, SRP must ensure customers have the ability to buy power 24-hours a day, seven-days a week. To facilitate that, SRP maintains relationships with several grocery store chains to host payment kiosks. During peak periods, SRP's 120 machines will handle 1.2 million transactions per month, mostly in cash.

The results of pre-pay are positive for the customer and for SRP. Pre-pay customers have the highest level of satisfaction of any customer segment. Customers combining pre-pay with in-home real-time energy displays are realizing a 12 percent reduction in energy consumption.

SRP acknowledges that there was initial pre-pay concern from social agencies. SRP worked carefully with these agencies to earn their trust. Customers are never forced on the program, and those with medical or transportation issues that make it difficult for them to visit a pay center to buy power are screened out. If customers are truly unable to pay, they are moved to credit billing and community resources are identified to help keep on their power.

Mike and his team have plans to take this service to the next level with a smart meter platform. This platform will allow customers to pre-pay and buy power without leaving their homes. Mike feels this change will increase the attractiveness of the program, and SRP will see greater adoption of pre-pay service.

Time-of-Use

SRP has also been innovative in their time-of-use offerings. Today, over 290,000 customers are enrolled in time-of-use (TOU) programs.

SRP started offering traditional TOU in the 1980s. Today, over 150,000 customers are enrolled in traditional time-of use tariff with a seven-hour on-peak period Monday through Friday in the summer and a bifurcated 10-hour on-peak period Monday through Friday in the winter.

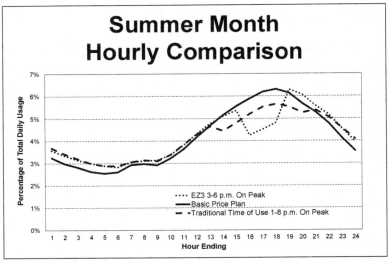

Fig. 7.3. SPR customers respond to price signals

SRP innovated the TOU offering with the introduction of EZ-3 in 2008 which it deployed to a pilot group of 15,000 customers. EZ-3 was made generally available in 2012, and today 140,000 customers participate in a more convenient, simpler offering. EZ-3 offers three timeslots during which customers are encouraged via pricing to curtail usage. The 3-hour time slots are Monday through Friday all year round, and they overlap each other. Customers can choose from slots that run from 2 pm–5 pm, or 3 pm–6 pm or 4 pm–7 pm. Customers participating on the EZ-3 demonstrate a dramatic drop in demand (Fig. 7-3.).

SRP has noticed substantial differences in the psycho-demographics between customers who choose the basic non-time differentiate plan, still the most popular pricing option chosen by over two-thirds of SRP's 900,000 customers, and other rate plans. Customers choosing this basic non-time differentiated option tend to be middle to lower income, single users who consume smaller amounts of energy. These customers tend not to be focused on the environment and are not big adopters of technology. Typically, these customers do not engage with SRP.

Customers choosing the traditional time-of-use program tend

to be families with high electricity usage. These customers tend to have higher incomes and be technology adopters. These customers are also highly engaged with SRP.

Consumers choosing the EZ-3 tend to be younger, single, mid to lower income consumers who are generally engaged with SRP. This group is also the most extensive adopter of technology.

SRP invested in smart meters in 2003. The higher costs to meter time-of-use customers made a strong business case for smart meters. With smart meters, a new suite of services became available to customers who now have the capability to receive bill estimates and see daily usage on the web. Soon, these users will be able to report an outage and receive confirmation via this platform. Mike believes SRP and its customers are just beginning to tap into the potential of the smart metering infrastructure.

WRAPPING IT UP

As Mike thinks about future utility customer service leaders, he advises that leaders should be willing to try new things. When an industry is as mature as the utility business is, Mike understands, thinking can be mired by past practices. Mike suggests, "Use the power of asking 'Why not?' to encourage innovation in thoughts and ideas."

"Use the power of asking 'Why not?' to encourage innovation in thoughts and ideas."—Mike Lowe

---

As the utility industry looks forward to the next 10 years, it sould expect challenges in dealing with the rising role of technology and increasing customer expectations. Further, Mike notes, "There will be questions about who owns the customer when it comes to providing energy management services and advice. Increasingly, more and more companies are entering this space and dealing directly with our utility customers."

REFERENCES

1.   Lowe, Mike. Interviewed by Penni McLean-Conner, November 30, 2015.

2.   Lowe, Mike. Follow Up on Questionnaire Responses, January 16, 2016 and January 20, 2016.

3.   "SRP Again Ranks Highest in West Among Residential Customers;" SRP press release, July 15, 2015; http://www.srpnet.com/newsroom/releases/071515.aspx

4.   Mendonca, Michael; Pratt, Jim; Traasdahl, Glen; Wisdom, Wayne; and Zittle, Cheryl. Interviewed by Penni McLean-Conner, March 16, 2016.

5.   Salt River Project; Facts About SRP; http://www.srpnet.com/about/facts.aspx

6.   Salt River Project; History of Salt River Project; http://www.srpnet.com/about/history/default.aspx

CHAPTER 8:

DAVID (DAVE) MCKENDRY, HYDRO OTTAWA

 **D**avid (Dave) McKendry[1] grew up in Ottawa, Canada and proudly leads customer service for Ottawa's municipal electric utility, Hydro Ottawa. Dave's authentic passion for the customer and excellence in leadership are cornerstones of his success. His strong core value system has allowed him to drive industry change while at the same time fulfilling family and community commitments.[2]

Interviews with Dave's direct reports, Marybeth MacDonald[3] and Michel Provost,[4] and Dave's boss Norm Fraser,[5] reveal a leader who places the customer at the center of everything—a leader with strategic vision who engages the team around him. Indeed, Dave's word cloud (Fig. 8-1), which is the visual representation of the words used to describe Dave in these interviews, shows the customer in the center, with customer experience and customer-centric also prominent. Strategic, leadership and ideas are words used to describe Dave's innovativeness. Value, engagement, employees, among others, are words that highlight his abilities to engage his team.

Fig. 8-1. Dave McKendry word cloud

Norm Fraser, Dave's boss, describes him, "Dave, an idea machine with a natural bent on strategic thinking, wears passion for the ideas on his sleeves." He credits Dave with "single-handedly ushering in the concept of customer experience," which today shares a laser-beam focus at Hydro Ottawa alongside Financial Strength, Organizational Effectiveness and Corporate Citizenship. Norm adds, "People naturally gravitate to Dave. He is articulate; he presents and speaks well."

> "Dave, an idea machine with a natural bent on strategic thinking, wears passion for the ideas on his sleeves."
> —Norm Fraser

Michel describes Dave as a catalyst who "walks the talk regarding the customer every day." He recalls one of the early initiatives Dave launched called the Customer Service Improvement (CSI) program, which proved to be an incubator for transforming the culture. The CSI program required that every employee go through Customer Service training. Michel remembers, "It allowed employees to look at our business from the customer's perspective and helped employees think about their role in serving the customer."

Marybeth talks about Dave's challenge to his team to continually try new things, and she wryly notes Dave's favorite questions include, 'Why do we do it this way?' and 'Is there a better way?' Importantly, Marybeth shares that Dave then allows his team to act on the ideas. He empowers them to implement. As an example of this, Marybeth describes Dave's vision behind MyHydroLink, Hydro Ottawa's customer service portal, which his team then implemented.

Rod Litke, Chief Executive Officer of CS Week, characterizes Dave as a leader who is constantly innovating. "A respected customer service visionary, Dave is leading Hydro Ottawa's drive to deliver value, both as a community asset providing essential services to the public and as an investment for its shareholder, the City of Ottawa," Rod shares.

All those interviewed note importantly that Dave is grounded in family, community and service. In fact, Dave has been involved with United Way for many years and serves on its Revenue Management Committee. The United Way is just one of many organizations in which Dave shares his passion for community service.

The word cloud highlights other descriptors like storyteller, ambassador, genuine and family, words that illustrate who and what make Dave McKendry tick. His profile further explores this proven leader, his career path and the drivers for those choices. Dave reveals the secrets of the "Killer B's and All About Me" which are fundamental to the success Hydro Ottawa enjoys while providing great service. Dave shares insights on how he develops and enables a customer-focused team and culture. He also offers advice to aspiring customer service leaders.

UTILITY OVERVIEW: HYDRO OTTAWA

Hydro Ottawa is a municipal electric utility serving Canada's capital city, Ottawa. This 130-plus-year-old utility has a proud history of providing low cost electric service and today serves over 325,000 customers.[6]

Hydro Ottawa originated in 1882 as the Ottawa Electric Company which provided electricity via Canada's first hydro-electric power plant. This company held many firsts including powering Canada's Parliament buildings with electricity a full year before electricity lit the US Capital buildings in Washington, DC. The utility also enabled Ottawa to become the first city in the world to illuminate all of its streets with electricity.

During the 1900s, the utility grew through a series of mergers with small town-based electric-generating plants and companies serving customers in and around Ottawa. In 2000, Hydro Ottawa was incorporated following a number of city amalgamations in the province of Ontario, including Nepean Hydro, Ottawa Hydro, Kanata Hydro, Gloucester Hydro, Goulbourn Hydro and the Town of Casselman.

Looking forward, Hydro Ottawa's mission is to create long-term value for their shareholder while benefitting their customers and the communities they serve.

Hydro Ottawa places the customer at the center of everything the utility does. It acknowledges that understanding and responding to customers' needs and expectations for quality service, cleaner energy and greater control over the management of energy costs will be the keys to Hydro Ottawa's continued success.[7]

CREATING A CUSTOMER-FOCUSED CULTURE

Dave points out, "Improving the customer experience is a journey, not a destination, and it starts from the top." Indeed, Dave credits Bryce Conrad, Hydro Ottawa's President and CEO for placing the customer directly in the bull's eye of the company's corporate strategic plan. "From top to bottom - from executive through management to our professional and dedicated staff - everyone seeks to serve our customers well. It is this support and vision from the top that guides the company through each step of the journey as we collectively move Hydro Ottawa's customer experience from good to great."

As the diagram illustrates, customer value is at the center of Hydro Ottawa's strategic plan (Fig. 8-2). As a key contributor, Dave is helping to architect the processes, metrics and technology that deliver on this core focus area.

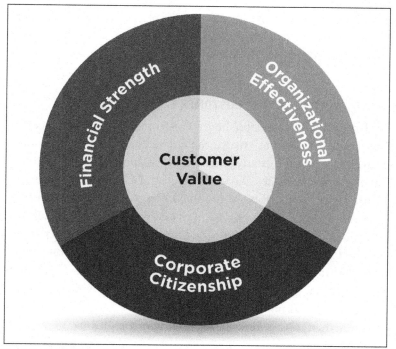

Fig. 8-2. Hydro Ottawa Customer Value Framework

Hydro Ottawa strives to be recognized by its customers and the electrical utility industry as a customer service leader. Its customer experience vision articulates the company's desire to be:

- Easy to do business with
- Caring
- Efficient
- Knowledgeable

As Director of Customer Service, Dave is a facilitator, working with a team of cross-functional executives who have conceptualized and who are now implementing Hydro Ottawa's customer experience vision. Hydro Ottawa is delivering on this mission by listening to the voice of the customer (VoC), through the development of customer personas and the creation of a company-wide Customer Experience Roadmap.

ORGANIZING FOR ALIGNED CUSTOMER EXPERIENCES

Hydro Ottawa has established a Customer Experience Steering Committee (CxSC) to ensure the entire enterprise is aligned on customer-focused initiatives. The CxSC is sponsored by the top of the house and includes Dave as Director of Customer Service and various executives who are involved directly and tangentially in customer service or the provision of enabling technologies. Other specialists are brought in as needed for subject matter expertise.

The CxSC provides oversight, coordination and direction to Hydro Ottawa's customer experience initiatives. To assist with this direction, a single, 'living' integrated, utility-wide Customer Experience Roadmap has been developed.

While the CxSC is new, its organizing principles establish ownership for the customer across the entire utility. The CxSC meets at least monthly to ensure projects and initiatives are prioritized, resourced and proceeding according to plan.

COMPLETING MARKET RESEARCH

Dave is a big proponent of truly understanding the customer base. To accomplish this, Dave led the foundational market research to develop Hydro Ottawa's customer personas. This six-month effort was supported by a consulting firm specializing in this work. The development of personas involved fully understanding who Hydro Ottawa's customers are, how they segment in multiple ways and how they interact with the utility.

Further, the research explored what messages resonated with each customer segment. To complete this research, Hydro Ottawa held a series of surveys with residential and small and medium business customers. It completed one-on-one meetings with large key accounts. It used customer focus groups to further refine the personas, engaging residential and commercial customers, contractors and developers.

Hydro Ottawa continues to maintain data on its six primary personas. It develops messaging and product and service offerings based on the attributes of these personas. A couple of examples portray two of the six personas:

- Penny Pinched is representative of 19 percent of Hydro Ottawa's residential customers. She is a single parent who owns a home and her family is dependent on her. Because money is tight, she lives financially month to month. Her day-to-day life is stressful and busy, with a lot of expenses.

- Sam Simplify on the other hand, represents 18 percent of Hydro Ottawa's residential customer base. He is a single, young professional who rents an apartment, is building his career, leads a simple life and doesn't worry about finances.

For each of its customer personas, Hydro Ottawa has gathered information that further describes each persona. These include relationship status and attitudes towards Hydro Ottawa, each persona's desired products and services from the utility and their preferred communications and messaging channels.

LISTENING TO THE VOC

Hydro Ottawa uses a variety of channels to hear the VoC. These include survey processes, complaint data analysis and employee feedback.

Survey Processes

Like many utilities, Hydro Ottawa surveys its customers. These surveys encompass transactional surveying, along with an annual general customer satisfaction survey.

Currently, Hydro Ottawa is completing transactional-based surveys triggered by a customer calling its call center. Dave has instituted a unique, low cost but substantive approach to this transactional survey. Each month, a random week including two days of calls is selected and those customers receive an outbound call from Hydro Ottawa asking for feedback. With its automated system, surveys require only two minutes of the customer's time. Customers rate service satisfaction in the following areas: speed of call answer, courtesy, knowledge, whether their question/concern was answered the first time and their overall experience. Where applicable, customers respond with yes or no answers or with ratings on a scale of 1 to 5 by pressing the phone key pad. The hit rate averages ten percent for the automated survey and has an associated cost of $300 per month.

There are plans to expand transactional research. Other areas to survey include power outage communications and restoration, field service work and tree-trimming work, among others.

Hydro Ottawa also administers an annual survey, similar in nature to J.D. Power's surveys, whose results are shared widely with management, from the CEO to Supervisors, so they can further communicate the results with all staff. This effort tunes the entire utility to what customers are thinking. Dave encourages all management to consider this VoC feedback when they develop their operational and strategic plans for the upcoming year.

Complaint Data

Complaint data is analyzed and used to improve performance. By mining complaints for process improvements, complaints have continued to decline. In fact, Hydro Ottawa has reduced complaints by 87 percent in a 10-year period, improving from over 2,100 annually to less than 300 per year. By establishing a dedicated, consistent team to resolve, track and analyze all complaints, Dave has instituted improvements in the customer complaint experience, whether they originate from the media, mayor or via escalation from the call center.

Feedback from Employees

Dave also relies on employee feedback on the customer experience to enhance processes. Whether from focus groups with frontline employees or one-on-one meetings with customer account executives, Dave and his team constantly ask for feedback, noting, "Employees like being asked. They bear a responsibility to be the VoC." And of course, this feedback identifies improvement opportunities. For example, a recent improvement to customer credit card payment options was introduced that now provides customers greater choice at a significant cost reduction, along with a much improved customer experience.

DEVELOPING LEADERS

Dave is not only passionate about enhancing his own leadership skills, but he spends time developing his entire customer service team to position them to achieve their best and, in turn, deliver on Hydro Ottawa's customer service mission. Dave's leadership strengths are personified through a combination of his background, mentors he has learned from and how he synthesizes these influences into his everyday communication style and processes. Dave's career path to becoming the customer leader for Hydro Ottawa is fascinating and instructive, and it demonstrates the importance of being grounded in core values.

Career Path

It is important to know that all of Dave's immediate family members are located in the Ottawa area. Dave is married to Karen, and together they have three children: Chelsea, Matt and Allie, plus two grandchildren. When asked about his family, Dave beams, "I am blessed!"

Home and family form the core of Dave's essence. His career path is unique in multiple dimensions. It spans both the telecommunications and electric utility sectors and has included positions based domestically and abroad. Some roles have played strongly on his innovative and entrepreneurial nature, while others leveraged his ability to execute a plan. Dave's job history demonstrates the importance of actively managing a career built upon a foundation of understanding what is most important to the individual. His career titles include everything from sales representative, to director, to vice president, to president and many in-between.

Dave graduated from Carleton University and holds a Bachelor of Arts degree and a Masters Certificate in Energy Sector Leadership from York University in Toronto. His introduction to his 'first real job' with Bell Canada came from a customer interaction when Dave worked as an in-home cable sales rep. Dave recalls presenting the cable package to an engaging and distinguished man who asked what he was planning to do for his career. The customer went on to say that if he were ever interested in Bell Canada to give him a call. Dave did. Turns out the gentleman, Larry Fox, a Bell Canada executive, helped Dave land his first professional job with Bell in 1982.

One of Dave's early successes with Bell Canada involved selling their iNET2000 product, an electronic mail system integrated with online database access, considered state-of-the-art at the time. Dave notes that he will never forget being only 27 years old and presenting the product to an intimidating room full of grey-haired judges. But Dave was persuasive, and Bell Canada successfully implemented a customized system for the Canadian Bar Association called CBANet.

As the saying goes, success breeds success. When the new service became more popular, Bell Canada wanted to expand to the United

States, and they asked Dave to take a key role in the new venture. So Dave moved to Virginia for this three-year commitment to build the business.

Even though strong competitors now shared this space, Dave was successful. At 30 years old, he secured a key sale to the American Bar Association. The team assisting Dave grew to over 100 employees and together they successfully orchestrated a seamless transition of 3,500 lawyers to ABANet. The US Supreme Court followed suit and called upon Dave and his team to assist them with their telecommunications requirements.

About this time, Dave was faced with a critical decision: stay with the US practice, which Bell Canada was officially spinning off to become a separate business unit, or return to Ottawa and continue with Bell Canada. Dave pondered this decision, and he considered Karen and their young family with first child, Chelsea, and his Dad in Canada who had been diagnosed with Parkinson's disease. Dave chose family.

Three years after returning to Ottawa with Bell, Dave was persuaded to take on a new and interesting role with Bell Canada International, exporting Bell's people and technologies to Australia and New Zealand. Dave accepted the Director of Sales and Marketing role and began commuting every few weeks to Australia, a 28-hour door-to-door trip with a 14 to 16-hour time zone shift, depending on the time of year. The good news was business was booming in Australia. The bad news was travel and time away from his family was brutal. Dave told Bell Canada that he was stepping down from this role. But Bell countered with another suggestion that he consider moving his family to Australia. This was a game changer.

So Dave, Karen and their three children moved to Australia. They rented their home in Ottawa, storing their belongings, and managed to pack their remaining possessions into four suitcases and six blue Rubbermaid boxes.

With suitcases, boxes and children in tow, Dave and Karen made the 28-hour journey to Australia. After 16 months there, the company invited Dave to move with his family to Singapore where they resided for a further two years. The Singapore business development assignment saw Dave traveling extensively throughout the Asia Pacific region, building success upon success. Dave describes this series of moves, "We were on a magic carpet ride, but even magic carpet rides must come to an end." As he considered his aging parents half-way around the world, he decided to return to Ottawa. It was an important time for his children to know their grandparents.

"We were on a magic carpet ride, but even magic carpet rides must come to an end."
—Dave McKendry

So Dave and his family moved back to Ottawa, with Dave continuing to work the international side of Bell Canada. While his home base was Ottawa, travel was still extensive. Dave describes the role as challenging because it required him to tap into his strategic vision, business strategy acumen, and his execution and communication skills. Regardless of the professional challenges though, travel still kept him away from his family.

Dave again returned to his core values, deciding to leave Bell Canada, and embraced his entrepreneurial skills. He entered the high-tech arena and during this four-year period even launched a business of his own. However, with the business uncertainty surrounding the events of September 11, 2001, and a young family to support, Dave sought an opportunity that could balance home life with workplace challenges. This opportunity was realized when he learned about a Key Account Coordinator opportunity at Hydro Ottawa. Although the Hydro job was less 'glamorous' than the international assignments, it was a solid one, and Dave was able to be home at night. This choice launched the start of a tremendous career for Dave at Hydro Ottawa, where he rose quickly through the organization to his current role. Reflecting on his career path, Dave offers this advice to other up and coming leaders, "Don't be afraid to take on challenges that may be daunting. Don't worry that you don't know it all. The journey is part of the experience. You will find yourself growing, learning and evolving."

Mentors

Not surprisingly, Dave shares that his mom and dad are two of his lifetime mentors. His mother, now in her 80s, was a flying instructor who started her career in the 1950s. She was the designated flight test examiner for the Canadian astronauts who participated in the space shuttle program. Dave tells the story of his parents' meeting and his mom teaching his dad to fly an airplane. His dad later became an air traffic controller, "A career that allowed him to tell her where to go," Dave says tongue firmly in cheek.

From his mom, Dave learned the lesson to always be encouraging; from his dad, he appreciated the aspect of quality. His dad was fond of reminding Dave, "If a job is worth doing, it's worth doing right."

As with strong leaders, there are many mentors. For Dave, this included Larry Fox, the Bell Canada executive who gave Dave his first professional job. Larry was recognized as a leader who truly connected with employees on his team. He engaged with staff by using management-by-walking-around long before it was a popular management principle.

Dave believes that treating people as you would like to be treated is so fundamental. This lesson he learned at a young age from Arden Brooks, owner of a large automotive parts and hardware retail chain store. Dave recalls a time when Mr. Brooks was considering where to move a display of tires. Instead of just ordering a move, Mr. Brooks asked one of the staff members whether the tires should remain where they were or be situated in another area of the store. The staff member weighed the choice and then recommended the tires be moved. Dave recalls Mr. Brooks engaged the team to make the decision, while at the same time getting the result he was seeking, a better tire display.

Dave also comments on one of his best bosses ever, Ray Byrne, whom he worked for in Canada and Sydney, Australia. From Ray, Dave learned the value of collaborating to develop a plan of action, giving 'rope' which could be pulled either way and, importantly, celebrating success along the journey.

Customer Service Team

Dave applies his authentic leadership style and passion for the customer as he directs Hydro Ottawa's $1 billion meter-to-cash business. His 60-plus employees and outsourced contact center team handle the traditional responsibilities of billing, call center, credit and collections, meter data services and customer experiences. They produce 4 million bills, handle more than 300,000 customer calls and process over 50,000 moves annually. Hydro Ottawa has a full deployment of smart meters and all customers subscribe to time-of-use rates. The advanced metering infrastructure (AMI) continues to evolve, enabling remote disconnects and connections along with analytics for power diversion investigation.

Dave recommends, "To effectively lead a customer service team, it is important to ensure that your key messages are being effectively communicated throughout the organization." To achieve this, Dave uses a combination of one-on-one weekly meetings with his direct reports, regular manager/supervisor meetings and all-staff gatherings to engage the entire group. Dave is a gifted communicator, and he works with his managers to identify key messages and integrate them into his regular team meetings.

Dave is a big fan of celebrating success, thus linking employees to Hydro Ottawa's mission of customer service. Awards for Teamwork, Integrity, Service and Excellence are officially presented annually. Dave is very proud that his team members have received the Hydro Ottawa President and CEO's Award for Innovation and Productivity on multiple occasions.

Dave loves to walk around and connect with his team. He knows them by name. He gains valuable insights on the successes and gaps in the service delivery processes by spending time with those on the front line. And importantly, the team relishes the opportunity to connect with Dave.

Individual contribution plans are created to prepare his leadership team for the next opportunities. These written plans include developmental goals. Additionally, the team continually reviews succession planning.

To assist with ongoing training, Dave's team has invested in state-of-the-art customer service training that is entirely electronic (e) learning-based. This off-the-shelf system has been customized to complement their customer information system (CIS). The training includes content and tests to ensure understanding. Users move through the job specific curricula at their own pace. Passing scores allow employees to move to the next module. The training system also provides management reports so progress can be monitored and managed.

DELIVER CUSTOMER-FACING PRODUCTS AND SERVICES

Dave notes that when he thinks about utility customer service, it boils down to seven words, "The Killer B's and All About Me." Dave shares that "The Killer B's" are Billing and Blackouts. And "All About Me" refers to customers being treated as individuals.

> "...Utility customer service, it boils down to seven words, 'The Killer B's and All About Me.'"
> —Dave McKendry

Hydro Ottawa has significantly transformed its customers' experiences over the past 10 years, building off an advanced grid platform equipped with AMI. Dave notes that when he took on the role of Director of Customer Service, customer service presented several opportunities for improvement. Dave provided these stats: "We had 16,000 pieces of unopened mail. Correspondence was 73 days behind schedule. The outage communications system was broken. We did not have E-commerce capability, and budget billing reconciliation had not been done for many customers for several years." Dave's initial focus was to triage and stabilize. He then worked with his team to develop the go-forward strategy. He engaged a consulting organization to help build the strategy, which encompassed extensive market research and product and service development. This effort was concurrent with the implementation of Hydro Ottawa's AMI.

Recognizing that customer experience improvement is a journey, not a destination, over a two-year timeframe, Dave and his team addressed the issues and realized the following progress:

- Outage Communications. They implemented an outage communications management system that won a Chartwell Best Practices Award.

- Call Center. Contact center service levels and first call resolution improved.

- Web. They implemented MyHydroLink, their customer portal. Corresponding customer satisfaction increased and 46 percent of customers have now registered for MyHydroLink.

- Billing. Seven years ago, customers received paper bills every other month. Today all customers are equipped with AMI, subscribe to time-of-use rates and receive their bills monthly, with 35 percent receiving them electronically.

Billing, the First Killer B

Billing is the first Killer B. Dave notes, "Customers want accurate and timely bills that are as low as possible." These expectations drive the customer strategy.

From a cost perspective, Hydro Ottawa's CxSC is consistently challenging itself on whether Hydro Ottawa is doing everything it can to keep costs low while servicing customers. They optimize their sourcing strategies and harness technology to maximize productivity. Projects now underway include: the implementation of an 'Omni-channel' contact center experience, bill presentment redesign, rationalization of the company's websites, further improvements to the outage communications system and additional engagement with key accounts, developers and contractors, to name a few. Hydro Ottawa also offers energy efficiency programs and has been doing so for over a decade. It has put forward residential programs to remove old, inefficient refrigerators and coupons for energy efficient compact fluorescent (CFL) and now light emoting diode (LED) lights. It has implemented a smart thermostat control system that allows Hydro Ottawa to reduce demand by cycling tens of thousands of air conditioners on and off at different times.

The AMI infrastructure has been a game changer in providing enhanced services to customers. This system collects 1,500 times more data than traditional meter reads to produce customer bills. The complexity of customer bills has increased, and the demand to produce the bills more quickly is escalating. Gone are the days where customers were willing to wait for the mail to receive their billing and consumption information. With time-of-use rates, customers want to understand their usage sooner and more frequently.

That is where the web portal, MyHydroLink (MHL), has proven to be so impactful. Customers can query their electricity usage hourly, daily and weekly, and this data is available by 8:00 am for the previous day. The portal also provides customers with weather trends. MHL offers high contrast views for the visually impaired commensurate with mandated display requirements. Hydro Ottawa, with AMI, offers innovative and valued services like 'Predict My Bill' and 'Bill Alert.' It also provides alerts for consumption, peak consumption and a payment reminder, all based on customer preferences.

Blackouts, the Second Killer B

Hydro Ottawa works diligently to keep the power on and in fact has improved its performance in both reducing the number and duration of outages, the second Killer B. A system reliability leader in the province of Ontario, Hydro Ottawa is challenged to keep ahead of the power outage curve on top of an aging infrastructure. When the power goes off, timely and accurate communication is essential.

Hydro Ottawa has invested in smart outage communications systems which can proactively and accurately inform customers that the utility is aware of the outage and the estimated time of restoration, along with other key elements like cause and the number of customers impacted.

Dave spearheaded an initiative to automate outage communications. This system, which integrates the customer database and the outage management system, provides outage messaging via Hydro Ottawa's interactive voice response system (IVR). The result is that average outage call duration has been reduced by 83 percent from 3 minutes to 30 seconds. Blocked calls have been virtually eliminated. This effort and its results won Hydro Ottawa the Chartwell 2010 Best Practices award for Outage Communications.

Hydro Ottawa recognizes the importance of providing customers outage information. It offers an outage map that indicates crew status and shows both planned and unplanned outages.

"All About Me"

Dave believes customers want the utility to deal with them in their individually preferred channel of choice. Dave has led the effort to understand and segment customers. By using identified personas like Penny Pinched, Sam Simplify and Greg Green among others, Hydro Ottawa works to understand choices and service options that customers value. Ideally, Dave wants to drill down to understand customers at an individual level.

Hydro Ottawa connects with its customers through multiple channels, and a responsive website design allows access from their device of choice. But the real game changer for personalizing service is MyHydroLink (MHL).

MHL serves as the gateway for electric billing. Hydro Ottawa has a 35 percent e-bill penetration.

It is not surprising that customers are using MyHydroLink. The portal offers customers a 'Time-of-Use' consumption calculator and a 'What If Calculator' so they can compare different rate options. The portal also allows customers to initiate moving and billing changes online. Hydro Ottawa's web portal provides profile choices, including language preference – either English or French. Additionally, customers take advantage of the proactive alert service to 'predict their bill,' with Dave noting, "This is one of the most valued services based on customer activity." The portal also offers account alerts such as for past due payments and for customer-preference alerts based on cost, consumption or peak consumption. And importantly, customers can access MHL via their computer or mobile device because the system is hardware agnostic.

ADVICE TO CUSTOMER SERVICE LEADERS

Dave is passionate about moving the utility customer's experience to the next level at Hydro Ottawa and across the industry. As such, Dave freely shares his advice and counsel to up-and-coming leaders and to the industry about the importance of understanding the changes with our customers, industry and technology. Dave's advice can be summed up simply, "Be informed." Saying that, Dave explains the criticality of understanding what customers are saying and knowing how well or poorly your utility is performing against customer expectations. He also notes that, "You can't manage what you can't measure."

From a customer perspective, Dave challenges leaders to anticipate customer demands. He reminds that customer demands are ever increasing and the reality is that customers will continually compare their utility experience to every other customer experience they have. Real success in delivering customer service comes from understanding these rising customer expectations and matching energy and service solutions to these expectations. A great example of this is the increased delivery of personalized information to customers in an automated fashion, such as on MyHydroLink.

The utility industry is changing, and Dave cautions that new entrants are looking to insert themselves between the utility and its customers. As such, it is increasingly important to design and manage a regulatory and operational model that is flexible to adapt to the changing marketplace.

Technology is rapidly changing. Dave advises that customer service leaders will be wise to understand and contemplate the impact of technology changes, especially the explosion of the internet of things (IoT). This advancement in technology brings both opportunities and challenges to how energy and service is provided to customers.

Dave's authentic passion for the customer and for excellence in leadership is obvious upon meeting him. As he successfully delivers on Hydro Ottawa's mission to create long-term value for its shareholders while benefitting the customers and communities it serves, Dave is also driving the entire industry to new levels. Dave serves on the board of directors of CS Week, is past Chair and an active member of the Canadian Electricity Association's Customer Council, and sits on the conference board of Canada's Customer Experience Council.

"Be informed." – Dave McKendry

REFERENCES

1. McKendry, David. Interviewed by Penni McLean-Conner, August 31, 2015.

2. McKendry, David. Follow Up Questions from Interview, October 2, 2015.

3. McDonald, Marybeth. Interviewed by Penni McLean-Conner, November 5, 2015.

4. Provost, Michel. Interviewed by Penni McLean-Conner, November 2, 2015.

5. Fraser, Norm. Interviewed by Penni McLean-Conner, January 14, 2016.

6. History of Hydro Ottawa; https://hydroottawa.com/about/our-company/our-history

7. History of Hydro Ottawa; https://hydroottawa.com/about/our-company/strategic -direction

CHAPTER 9:
JOSEPH (JOE) TRENTACOSTA,
SOUTHERN MARYLAND ELECTRIC COOPERATIVE

As Senior Vice President of Customer and Enterprise Services and Chief Information Officer for Southern Maryland Electric Cooperative (SMECO), Joseph (Joe) Trentacosta has his hands full.[1] But he would not have it any other way. Today's reality is that information technology (IT) is a key service provider to enable the customer experience. Joe loves the fact that, tasked with both roles, he holds the unique position to be both service provider and client. And the combination works well for delivering excellent customer service. In fact, with Joe's leadership, J.D. Power has ranked SMECO highest in customer satisfaction among midsize utilities in the East region for eight years in a row.[2]

Joe came to the energy industry by way of telecom. This background honed Joe's ability to embrace change, understand and implement complex IT solutions and develop a talented, engaged team. Under Joe's leadership, SMECO has been successful in establishing a robust IT platform. This engine powers their customer service delivery and has positioned SMECO to engage their customer-members via multiple channels in a seamless manner.

Joe's profile explores leadership from dual perspectives: his unique career path and how he develops his team. Joe shares insights on how his team uses and analyzes data to enhance the customer experience. And the profile reveals how Joe continually keeps up with customer-members' increasing expectations by delving into some of SMECO's customer-facing products and services.

JOE TRENTACOSTA OVERVIEW

When interviewing Joe's direct reports and his boss, several themes emerged regarding his leadership style. Joe's management team includes: Tami Gardiner, Credit and Collections Director; Rose Pickeral-Brown, Vice President Customer Care; Dave Viar, Reliability, Compliance and Security Managing Director; and Sylvia Welch, Managing Director of Information Technology.[3] Joe's boss is Joe Slater,[4] the Chief Executive Officer of SMECO. The word cloud (Fig. 9-1) highlights the dual roles around the customer and information technology which are front and center. Joe's leadership style is characterized as calm, with a deliberate approach and grounded in integrity. He is very much involved with his team and serves as an advisor.

Joe's leadership of both the IT and customer service operations is evident in the interviews. Significant descriptors of internal and external customer are frequently referenced by his team, who note that Joe ensures a 'focus on the internal and external customer.' Sylvia observes, "Joe is always looking to enhance service to customers." Tami shares, "Joe has great vision, and he continually looks to enhance process and systems to improve customer interaction."

The word survey shows up because of the intense focus Joe places on listening to customer feedback via surveys. The team notes that not only are survey results reviewed monthly, but if a rating is 3

Figure 9-1. Joe Trentacosta word cloud

or below on a scale of 1 to 5, Joe digs to understand why and then challenges the team to identify ways to improve.

From an IT perspective, Joe is ever seeking ways to use technology to get work done more quickly. His team shares that Joe likes to investigate and understand what is happening from an IT perspective. He is described as clever and quick to understand. The survey aspect applies to IT too because internal client surveys are completed and reviewed with the same discipline as external customer surveys.

Everyone uses the word calm to describe Joe. Words such as steady and unflappable are also shared. Joe combines a deliberate approach with this calm demeanor. Slater says, "Joe is unflappable. He wraps himself around a problem and attacks it in a calm and deliberate manner." Slater also observes that this characteristic is incredibly important in an IT group since decisions made in an excited environment could have huge consequences.

Joe also empowers others. He holds a level of trust in his team and employees that empowers them to act. With empowerment, though, comes accountability. Joe holds himself and his team accountable.

Joe brings core values and integrity to all that he does. And from this integrity comes trust. Rose shares, "Joe has trust in you and puts trust in his team." Dave adds, "Joe trusts me to get the job done." This foundation of trust coupled with Joe's core values provides the team with solid leadership. Dave notes, "Joe is trustworthy; he walks the talk and whether you like it or not, you can respect him for his stance ... I think it is important having someone you can trust and who has good character."

Dave shares that, with this trust, Joe can be counted on to make decisions. The word decisive is frequently mentioned. Particularly in the compliance and security responsibilities that Joe now holds, there are tough decisions to make. They require decisiveness. This courage to make decisions plays out in his profile, as Joe has been faced with some significant IT systems decisions in order to provide great service for customer-members.

The interviewees often referenced Joe's role as an advisor or consultant. This is linked with Joe's natural desire to be actively engaged. Because he is approachable, employees at all levels feel comfortable talking to him and find that he listens and rolls up his sleeves to get involved. Slater shares, "Joe's personal style and demeanor make employees feel very comfortable asking for advice." Sylvia adds, "When someone has an issue, Joe makes an effort to investigate and make sure he fully understands what needs to be done." Joe is involved, and he works best one-on-one.

Other words that Joe's staff and boss used to describe him include family. Joe is grounded in his family and community. He has vision and really enjoys working with employees. Slater sums up, "Joe is a person of high values and high moral fabric. The man behind the professional is highly devoted to his wife, family, parents, church and community."

UTILITY OVERVIEW: SOUTHERN MARYLAND ELECTRIC COOPERATIVE

SMECO serves over 160,000 customers in southern Maryland. This proud 80-year-old organization is centered on the customer-member. A nonprofit utility owned by customer-members, it is one of the largest electric cooperatives in the nation.

Electric cooperatives were started during the 1930s. This was after the First World War, and the United States was building its industrial strength, powered by electricity. On May 11, 1935, President Franklin Roosevelt signed Executive Order 7037 establishing the Rural Electrification Administration. This became the foundation for communities across rural America to organize and establish electrical service to their residents.

In 1935, Southern Maryland was sparsely populated and, as a result, investor-owned electric power companies were not interested in expanding their service to the area. Local citizens took matters into their own hands. They formed committees to seek federal assistance through the Rural Electrification Administration. On February 5, 1937, the Southern Maryland Tri-County Cooperative Association, later named the Southern Maryland Electric Cooperative, Incorporated was formed.

SMECO grew through the 1940s and 1950s by expanding to Calvert County. Today Southern Maryland is a highly popular suburb of Washington, DC.[5]

CREATING A CUSTOMER-FOCUSED CULTURE

A customer-focused culture is woven into the fiber of SMECO because it is owned by customer-members. Joe notes, "There is a laser-focus on customer service. There is no conflict on whether you are going to please the customer or the shareholder because they are one and the same. And the focus on customer service is shared by everyone from the board of directors, to line technicians, to customer service representatives. It is the culture."

> "There is a laser-focus on customer service..."
> —Joe Trentacosta

Modeling Passion for the Customer

Joe is a passionate role model for this focus on the customer. An enthusiastic cheerleader, he celebrates great customer service. He advocates for the customer-member and personally engages to resolve issues. He supports and empowers his team to deliver.

Celebrating Great Service

Joe and his team show appreciation and provide recognition to their team members for great customer service as a constant cycle, not once or twice a year. Recognition and incentive programs are intrinsic parts of the culture.

In a very personal way, Joe recognizes individual contact center representatives (CCRs) for connecting positively with the customer. For each customer compliment in which a CCR is called out by name, Joe sends an email to the responsible CCR, acknowledging and thanking them for the great service to reinforce the customer-focused behavior. It is not uncommon for Joe to send several dozen personal emails during a typical year, such as the email to James (Fig. 9-2).

Customer Survey Comment
Trentacosta, Joe
To: Hawkins, James C.
Cc: Rose.Pickeral@smeco.coop, Susan.Norris@smeco.coop, Huffin, Marsha, Swann, Dianna, Tana.Hill@SMECO.coop, Tanner, Tammy
Date: 12/5/2014 10:32:00 AM

James,

This morning we conducted our monthly customer survey review meeting, and one of our customers had the following nice comment about her interaction with you: "The gentleman, James, was very courteous and knowledgeable. Although a follow-up was not required, James called the next day to inform me my payment had been credited".

Well done, James! Thanks for going the extra mile, and thanks for providing great service to our customers each and every day.

Joe T.
Joe Trentacosta SMECO
Senior VP & CIO (240) 528-9752
Joe.Trentacosta@smeco.coop

Figure 9-2. Joe Trentacosta email highlighting the great service provided by James

Joe and his leadership team involve employees in designing recognition programs to achieve critical customer performance metrics. These metrics include call service levels and adherence to schedule, among others. Interestingly, the leadership team started out by trying to develop the program themselves, quickly realizing that CCRs would have the best ideas. So Joe challenged CCRs to develop a list of incentives that would motivate them. Believe it or not, the one that rose to the top and was implemented offered the chance to simply wear jeans every day for a month. It turned out to be a win-win incentive program for all.

Advocate for the Customer

At heart, Joe is a problem solver and likes to get involved in resolving customer issues. In the world today, many customer issues can be resolved through technology. Having responsibilities for both IT and customer service, Joe enjoys experiencing the lifecycle of problem identification and solution. His personal drive to really get involved in resolving customer issues is important to Joe's ability to set a tone of customer service.

Joe shared an example from 2011 when a customer complained that SMECO did not offer customers the ability to pay the bill using an online payment system through the bank. At the time, Joe acknowledged SMECO had received other inquiries about this service offering, but this particular customer punctuated his complaint by sending an email to Joe and SMECO's chief financial officer. Joe responded to the customer, advising him that SMECO was looking into this service offering. The customer thanked Joe for the response but mentioned he had contacted SMECO over three years before and heard a similar response. The customer also stated he represented the desires of many SMECO customers, not just himself.

Joe recalls this particular event triggered SMECO to re-prioritize eBill to the front burner. Indeed, one year later SMECO went live with an eBill solution. And, characteristic of Joe, he personally reached out to the customer letting him know the service was avail-

able. The customer was thrilled that SMECO had remembered and
followed up with him.

Empowerment

Joe also believes a culture of empowerment is critical to delivering
great customer service. Through its processes, guidelines and rules
for engaging customer-members, SMECO empowers its representatives to satisfy customers on the first call. Joe notes, "The leadership team and I really promote and reinforce the message that
CCRs are empowered, within reason, to satisfy the customer on
the first call. They do not have to gain approval from a supervisor."

But sometimes customers' problems are not resolved on the first
call. When that happens, the voice of the customer (VoC) provides
visibility into these slips via complaints, customer survey feedback
or phone call analysis. To guarantee customer issues are resolved,
Joe engages Senior CCRs in the process. They ensure CCRs follow
up in a timely manner, or Senior CCRs respond directly to customers if the CCR is unable to do so. Senior CCRs are also responsible
for training CCRs and for managing and updating customer service
procedures and processes. By assigning the Seniors this responsibility of ensuring customer issue resolution, they also find and
implement training and procedural enhancements that mitigate
repeat issues.

Organizing for Aligned Customer Experiences

Joe has organized his team to deliver great service and to empower
great service via IT. His team of over 100 individuals includes customer-facing services of the contact center, credit and collections
and field services, with corresponding IT services of application
management, infrastructure management and security.

To deliver the customer-facing services, Joe manages the vice
president of customer care and the director of credit and collections, retail choice and field services. The vice president of
customer care is responsible for the oversight and operation of

SMECO's 24/7 contact center. Reporting to the vice president position are managers in charge of the contact center, workforce management and specialists for training, quality assurance and speech analytics.

The director of credit and collections, retail choice and field services manages the traditional corporate credit and collections functions and the field services team. Since SMECO does not have an advanced metering infrastructure, the field team completes customer-requested turn-ons and turn-offs, along with field collection activities.

The managing director of IT oversees all IT functions, including automated business systems such as meter data management (MDM), financials and the customer information system (CIS). This position is also responsible for the corporate local-area networks, wide-area networks, data centers, telecommunications systems and various computing devices.

Additionally, the director of reliability, compliance and security is responsible for the Electric Reliability Internal Compliance Program (ICP) which includes North American Electric Reliability Corporation (NERC) and Critical Infrastructure Protection (CIP) compliance, information and cyber security, physical security, emergency response planning, records retention and eDiscovery.

Hiring the Right Team Members

As Joe continues to grow and build his team, he notes four critical skill sets he looks for in prospective customer service team members: customer service, multitasking, teamwork and flexibility. "Fundamentally, they must have customer service skills that come naturally," Joe says, "And beyond customer service, today's employees need to be able to multitask." Joe recognizes that in frontline customer service, staff turnover trends higher than in other areas of the utility. Characteristic of Joe, he leverages technology to help find the right team members. He recognizes that CSRs while on the phone with customers may multitask to monitor both the CIS and outage management system (OMS) simultaneously,

To more efficiently screen potential CSR candidates, Joe implemented an online screening tool to assess customer service capability. The tool is presented to prospective employees via an email containing a hyperlink. The candidate has five days to complete a simulation which assesses and scores both customer service and multitasking abilities, via the internet. Candidates scoring 75 percent or above proceed to the next step in the hiring process.

> "Fundamentally, they must have customer service skills that come naturally."—Joe Trentacosta

Additionally, Joe looks for evidence of teamwork and flexibility in prospective employees. Knowing great service delivery takes a group effort, SMECO has aligned an entire team of people for each service offering, often from different departments to ensure the service is delivered timely and with quality. Joe understands how important it is for customer service employees to have the ability to function as a team, share ideas and feedback and work together to create a great customer service experience.

Flexibility is also important. Employees must be open to change. The message about flexibility starts from the first day a prospective employee meets with SMECO. The co-op's call center management team, supervisors, directors and managers emphasize flexibility. If prospective employees are inflexible and unable to adapt to change, the SMECO environment is not for them. In addition to system changes, regulations are always changing which means customer service changes to meet ever increasing customer service needs. Joe advises, "SMECO is not a good workplace fit if you want to sit and do the same thing year after year."

> "SMECO is not a good workplace fit if you want to sit and do the same thing year after year."
> — Joe Trentacosta

Listening and Measuring the VoC

As with all great customer-focused organizations, the VoC plays a prominent role. SMECO captures member feedback via random surveys, customer complaint data analysis and social media trends, among others.

SMECO conducts monthly random customer surveys as an overall metric to understand how service is meeting the overall needs of members. These surveys are paper-based and ask customers to rate the initial contact and follow-up. The corporate communications team manages this process. Data is shared broadly to the entire organization.

And like any 21st century utility, SMECO uses social media to keep tabs on quickly changing customer sentiment and feedback. SMECO's social media specialist monitors the corporate Facebook page and responds quickly to relevant posts. Whether complaining about high energy bills following record-breaking temperatures during a cold January or joining the conversation after a widespread weather-related outage, the two-way communication between SMECO and its customer-members provides invaluable feedback. SMECO uses social media to promote new programs and to warn customers about phone scams. When door-to-door solicitors claiming to work for SMECO sparked some anxiety among customer-members, they were reported to the co-op. A SMECO Facebook post cautioning homeowners to beware garnered more than 2,500 shares and reached nearly 96,000 people.

SMECO also measures its performance with customers. Indeed, corporate key performance indicators are tied to SMECO's strategic imperatives. Annual compensation and bonus plans are based on whether or not SMECO achieves specific performance goals. Metrics are regularly published and reviewed.

There are four key metrics that provide a top tier view of the customer and the service. These are inbound call service levels, call abandonment rates, customer satisfaction survey results from the initial contact and follow-up. While there are other important operational metrics supporting these top tier ones, these four are reviewed regularly by the CEO and his team. In turn, the CEO includes these metrics in a monthly progress report shared with the SMECO Board of Directors.

DEVELOPING LEADERS

Joe's role as Senior Vice President of Customer and Enterprise Services and Chief Information Officer (CIO) for SMECO is rather unique in the industry. Joe brings strong IT experience to this role, along with the understanding of fast-paced growth and development gained from a decade in the telecommunications industry. To this foundation, he has developed a strong understanding of core utility meter-to-cash processes so critical to consistently delivering great customer service. Joe notes, "When I took on the responsibility for customer service after years of being an information technology (IT) professional, I did not know what I was in for. It was a real opportunity to broaden my focus from satisfying internal customers to satisfying both internal and external customers. The enjoyment I got from satisfying customers from my many years in IT translated naturally into this new role which combined both. This role has given me a great appreciation for the ultimate vision for the co-op, having direct responsibility for the customers. And I finally get to see the impact of operational decisions on our customers. This is very powerful and motivating."

Joe's career path serves as an instructional guide on how to successfully balance, develop and broaden one's skills and experiences, while also staying grounded in core values. Joe is the leader he is today because of important career experiences and advice from mentors. And as a savvy leader, Joe also focuses on building leaders who surround him.

Career Path

Joe owns a fascinating background rich in IT experience. In fact, Joe started in telecom in the information technology department, which in the 1980s was called management information systems

(MIS). Joe began in 1985 when the cellular industry was in its infancy, and companies were building out their first networks.

Joe landed his first professional job with Metro Mobile in New York City in the 1980s. The business was fast paced, and Joe remembers, "To be successful, you had to embrace change." Metro Mobile, a pioneer in the cellular industry, owned networks in the northeast, southeast and southwest United States. But like many burgeoning new industries, Metro Mobile was purchased by Bell Atlantic Mobile, so Joe transitioned to Bell Atlantic Mobile's corporate headquarters in Bedminster, New Jersey.

As Bell Atlantic optimized its organization, Joe was offered a promotion to a director role in information technology in the Washington, DC and Baltimore region. Single at this point in time, Joe recognized this move would provide him the ability to rapidly advance his career. He accepted on the spot without even visiting the area. And he was quickly promoted to executive director. The fast-paced growth of the cellular industry presented a wonderful opportunity for Joe to gain experience and skills quickly.

"To be successful you had to embrace change."
—Joe Trentacosta

Joe grew both personally and professionally in the Baltimore area. In fact, he met his wife Mary, and they married in 1998. Joe, Mary and her two sons grew roots in Maryland, and their family was completed with the birth of their daughter. Providing their family with a life that supported both professional development and a love for their community was important to Joe and Mary.

So when Bell Atlantic reorganized and offered Joe a position back in New Jersey, Joe was faced with a great career move but one that required uprooting his family. Because family is a core value to Joe, the right answer for him and his family was to decline.

Joe now began a search for a new job. As he hunted, Joe broadened his perspective to include utilities, understanding the service nature of utility and telecom industries shared similar business models of supporting customers using technology.

Concurrent to Joe's job search, SMECO had recently announced its new CEO, Joe Slater. Faced by some serious obstacles in his new role, Slater began his tenure with a challenged CIS implementation, which SMECO had embarked on five years earlier in anticipation of customer choice being offered in Maryland. Realizing the importance of IT to serving his members, Slater began a search for SMECO's first CIO.

Joe loves telling the story that he learned about the SMECO CIO position vacancy by reading the want ads in the newspaper. While Joe considered responding to a newspaper ad an unlikely way to land a job, he submitted his resumé. Joe was one of more than 900 candidates who applied, but with Joe's strong IT background from the fast-paced cellular industry, he was hired.

It was a smooth transition for Joe from telecom to the utility business. He learned industry nomenclature and its unique IT systems like the supervisory control and data acquisition (SCADA) systems used by utilities to monitor electrical assets and OMS. Plus, Joe arrived at SMECO familiar with other important and common IT systems supporting financials, human resources and supply chain.

Joe's first goal was to take the CIS system live, and he did. It was a challenged project labeled as 'over budget and delayed.' But in six months, Joe brought the system into production status. The CIS system was live and working but heavily customized and unsupported. SMECO was one of two clients of the CIS vendor. Specialists who supported the system were traveling from Australia. SMECO was spending tons of resources trying to maintain the system, and Joe realized this status was unsustainable.

Joe recalls, "I had to make a bold decision," so he walked into the CEO's office and said, "Joe, we need to replace the CIS." And they did. Even though SMECO had spent a great deal of time and money on the CIS, Joe and the CEO prepared the case to the board of directors, convincing them that change was needed. Joe received the support he requested, and over the next eighteen months, he led the implementation of a new minimally-customized CIS, delivered on time and on budget. The new CIS was a great implementation and enjoyed flawless execution. It demonstrated the merits of excellent teamwork and strong executive support. Joe proudly points to SMECO's extremely talented and educated IT team for the implementation success.

"I had to make a bold decision."—Joe Trentacosta

The implementation of the CIS helped Joe build a strong understanding of customer service processes. So it seemed natural to SMECO for Joe to add the customer service organization to his role as CIO. In 2008, Joe took on the additional responsibilities of the contact center. His title changed to Senior Vice President Customer and Enterprise Services and CIO. Joe notes, "The beauty of this role is that I oversee both IT and customer service. I am my own client. This works well."

Mentors

When exploring the important role of mentoring, Joe shares that mentors have provided him with insight and wisdom, qualities he has incorporated into his career. Joe fondly recalls his father, a role model for everything in his life. Joe's dad was all about family and doing the right thing for his children with honesty and integrity. Growing up and observing his dad, Joe vowed, "If I ever become a father or a leader, I need to be dedicated and focused on my family, my job, my organization and on the people who work for me." Joe strives to give his very best every day he walks into the office.

As with many successful leaders, Joe has learned from many talented folks. He identifies traits of leaders he works with and integrates them into his leadership style. For example, Slater, SMECO's CEO, displays an effortless style of inclusiveness. When Slater wants to make a decision, he assembles people and builds consensus. The CEO has the ability to make everyone feel a part of the process. And most of the time, Joe notes, "Everyone feels good about the final decision and, if they do not, at least they understand they were a part of the process."

Joe candidly offers that he learned lessons from bad leaders too. For example, Joe is committed to never embarrassing an employee in front of other people. He adopted this lesson early on because a boss did just that to Joe publically. Joe noted that he vowed never to use that tactic himself. "It is so important to treat people with dignity and respect," he says. "That is how I conduct myself as a leader and a manager."

Developing Customer Service Leadership

Joe is driven to develop his leadership team. He relies on two core processes for this development: challenging projects and continuous learning.

Challenging projects. Joe loves challenging his leaders with new projects. For example in 2008, SMECO began implementing a suite of workforce automation tools, which ultimately won the CS Week Expanding Excellence Award in 2014. As SMECO rolled out various automation tools over the years, including computer telephony integration (CTI), e-learning and advanced scorecards, he asked various team leaders to implement these products. These projects developed leaders and honed their collaboration, business execution and project management skills.

Continuous learning. Joe encourages his leadership team to always grow and develop. He nudges leaders to secure certifications and additional education and to keep abreast of industry best practices, trends and developments. He uses cross-training to build a broader understanding of SMECO's systems. Joe also encourages talent to keep current in today's rapidly changing energy landscape. He and his leaders take time to meet with technology vendors who provide insight on the latest technology projects and offer product roadmaps on how the technology may integrate with SMECO's business plans.

Industry conferences offer another important source for insights, best practices and networking. Joe himself attends a select few, like CS Week. The overflow interactive voice response (IVR) system installed at SMECO today, for example, was the result of a discussion Joe shared with a customer service vice president a few years ago at an industry meeting.

Cross-training is important for two reasons. It helps leaders understand the various elements and drivers of the meter-to-cash cycle. It also creates a leadership team that understands how the entire business/technology process works in harmony.

For cross-training, Joe has contact center and credit and collection personnel switch jobs. Contact center folks working in credit and collections enjoy the opportunity to spend time in the field watching the disconnect process. These leaders also spend time in the credit office hearing firsthand the outbound collection and payment calls. This helps paint the big picture. Similarly, for credit leaders, time in the contact center exposes them to the technologies and processes needed to successfully manage a large inbound call center. These leaders gain exposure to the wide variety of customer inquiries along with the challenge of keeping a team motivated when handling call after call after call.

DELIVER CUSTOMER-FACING PRODUCTS AND SERVICES

SMECO has been rated at the top of J.D. Power rankings for the past eight years. Not by chance, this effort has been a deliberate business strategy, leveraging the strong IT infrastructure to continually optimize the customer service team. To that end, Joe is very excited about the success of offering customer-members mobile-based tools and, particularly, the process improvement potential of SMECO's new speech analytics tool.

Mobile-Based Tools

SMECO has long recognized that customer service was moving to electronic platforms. To that end, SMECO invested in its first electronic bill payment and presentment platform in 2004 with great success. The system was grounded in customer feedback, and the rollout used the soft launch approach to begin the offering. Today, this electronic billing and payment platform, along with the OMS, serves as the foundation for new mobile-based tools.

In 2013, SMECO started the rollout of a series of mobile-based tools to enhance the customer-member experience. The first, outage reporting via two-way text messaging, was deployed in December 2013. The soft launch provided SMECO valuable feedback they used to adjust internal business processes, which also informed later mobile-based services. One example occurred during major outage events when, occasionally, services were energized via the OMS in an attempt to identify nested outages. With the new mobile-based outage tools, this practice was initiating power restoration text messages to customers who had signed up for the service. This mislead and confused customers who were still out of service. So, Joe explained, "The enhanced visibility associated with the new text-based outage tools drove us to modify this business process."

Also in late 2013, SMECO launched its mobile application called SMECO 24/7. To provide this, SMECO partnered with a recognized and leading utility mobile app provider. The mobile application offered customer-members another way to interact with SMECO via their mobile devices. Truly developed for people on the go, the app delivers a much quicker user experience. In addition to outage reporting capabilities, the app provides links to SMECO's social media pages (Twitter and Facebook). Per J.D. Power,[6] customer satisfaction is higher across all factors when customers are aware their utility offers a mobile app.

In 2014, SMECO continued its investment in mobile technologies by rolling out billing and payment alerts via text. When SMECO first offered a soft launch in December 2014, they were amazed 134 accounts had signed up for the service in a short 30 days. Feedback from these early adopters was so positive. Sign up has continued with more than 6,000 account enrollments for text-based services within eight months of the launch.

The sign up process is simple. Once enrolled, when the bill is ready, the customer-member receives a text. The customer-member can look at a mobile version of the bill and in three simple steps pay it. First, the customer texts, 'Pay.' Then, they are prompted to text a unique four-digit PIN established in a virtual wallet which links to the automated clearing house (ACH) information. This provides a secure payment transfer that connects to all US financial institutions. Finally, customers simply answer, 'Yes,' to authorize payment when prompted, and their electric bill is paid.

Speech Analytics

Joe is always looking to further optimize the customer-member's call experience. He is encouraged by early results of a new tool implemented which provides speech analytics. Speech analytics, a sophisticated conversational analytics tool, automatically identifies, groups and organizes words and phrases spoken during calls into themes, helping to reveal rising trends and areas of opportunity or concern.

The process works this way. Every single call is recorded, and the speech analytics tool looks for key words or phrases that SMECO has identified or categories that are pre-built. The system SMECO installed came 'out of the box' with an emotions category, which included words and phrases like 'really upset,' 'frustrated,' 'you people,' and 'not happy.'

One early success impacted repeat calls. Through this speech analytics tool, SMECO found out that customers were confused by the budget portion of the bill. Customer-members were calling because they did not understand how their energy usage and monthly payment should be displayed on budget billing. This invaluable information is being used now to inform how SMECO communicates and messages on budget billing.

Additionally, speech analytics has been instrumental in attacking repeat calls and customer confusion, the highest trending categories found by the tool. As SMECO captured and analyzed the calls that fell into those two categories, they found that many calls were centered on high bill inquiries. As they listened, SMECO realized that its CCRs were pacifying customer-members with meter read rechecks and meter tests instead of educating customers on their usage. This led to customer confusion and call backs.

As a result of the speech analytics, SMECO adjusted processes and provided re-training. The result has been a reduction in repeat calls in this space, but admittedly there is more to do. SMECO has hired a full-time analyst to manage this tool, identify insights and recommend corrective actions.

WRAPPING UP WITH INSIGHTS

Delivering great customer-member service is simply the SMECO way. SMECO has an unrelenting customer focus. Joe notes, "Our customers own us. It is all about them. We are not here without them. We are here to serve."

The SMECO leadership team realizes that an aggressive IT strategy is fundamental to serving a rapidly changing and increasingly digital customer base. While Joe admits that during the early 2000s SMECO lagged on IT systems, in the past 10 years, they have implemented over 20 business systems, including CIS, geographic information systems (GIS) and OMS. SMECO has embraced technology and is trending ahead of the curve. SMECO's strategy continues to be aggressive with technology, as evidenced by investments in speech analytics and mobile-based services.

Joe's success in steering SMECO's aggressive IT strategy and successfully leveraging it as his own client in the customer service team has been a recipe for outstanding customer satisfaction.

Joe is excited about the talented new leaders coming into the utility customer service space. His advice for these leaders? "Have courage in decision making," Joe reiterates, "It is okay if every decision is not a home run. You can be successful hitting singles and doubles occasionally. But it is important that leaders act decisively and move forward. Be courageous in your decision making; be bold."

"Be courageous in your decision making; be bold."
—Joe Trentacosta.

REFERENCES

1. Trentacosta, Joe. Interviewed by Penni McLean-Conner, September 16, 2015; Follow up questionnaires and materials, September 23, 2015 and October 15, 2015.

2. SMECO Awards and Commendations; https://www.smeco.coop/news/jd-power-2015.

3. Gardiner, Tami; Pickeral-Brown, Rose; Welch, Sylvia; Viar, Dave. Interviewed by Penni McLean-Conner, March 2, 2016.

4. Slater, Joe. Interviewed by Penni McLean-Conner, December 21, 2015.

5. History of Southern Maryland Electric Cooperative; https://www.smeco.coop/about/history

6. J.D. Power, February 2014 titled, "Mobile Customer Interaction 2014"

CHAPTER 10:
LOOKING FORWARD

C learly, these utility chief customer officers are successful at placing the customer as the central focus of their utilities. But all these leaders agree change is coming. Because of that inevitability, they are reflecting on and planning for a rapidly-changing landscape while positioning their utilities to serve customers in a meaningful manner with valued products and services. To that end, these CCOs have shared their thoughts on how rising customer service leaders can best prepare for these changes. They address shifts that will surely impact the utility industry, the workforce, technology and, most importantly, our customers.

INDUSTRY

Changes are afloat for the gas, electric and water industries. Thoughtful and careful understanding of these changes and their implications on the business model are needed to ensure customers continue to enjoy reliable, secure energy and water service at a reasonable cost.

Lisa Jacobson, Business Council for Sustainable Energy President states, "2015 clearly marked a turning point for American energy. As we consider the world in a post-Paris Agreement on climate change, we should acknowledge that the United States has also entered a new era for low-carbon energy." This new era carries significant implications on an energy delivery system that was designed for one-way flow. Energy delivery systems must now evolve to support two-way flow, increased renewables, electrification of transportation and the overall effort to decarbonize our energy sources.

Similarly, the natural gas industry is undergoing a transformation. In the *Natural Gas Utilities Playbook*, published by the American Gas Association, Dave McCurdy, President and CEO of the American Gas Association notes, "We have an abundance of clean natural gas in this nation that analysts predict will likely be available at affordable and stable prices for decades into the future. Millions of Americans see the benefits of natural gas every day, and 37 states have adopted or are currently considering innovative pipeline expansion proposals to deliver gas to communities that do not have it."

The landscape is also changing in the water industry where increased water scarcity, climate volatility and aging infrastructure are paramount concerns. Indeed, the water industry is transforming. The 2016 State of the Water Industry Report, produced by the American Water Works Association, highlights the challenges resulting from these changes. These include the public's understanding of the value of water systems, services and resources, along with the need to address aging water and wastewater infrastructure, to name just two.

Leaders in the electric, gas and water industry are actively discussing the role of the utility in the evolving energy and water landscape and the impacts of this transformation on the infrastructure, our customers and systems management. These leaders recognize this change represents opportunity as well.

Joanne Fletcher, Burbank Water and Power, is concerned, "There is not enough discussion on how to restructure to see how to bear costs equitability. It takes thoughtful consideration and most customers are not willing to engage in the conversation."

Marilyn Caselli, Con Edison, also acknowledges, "The utility industry is facing uncertainty right now, and the basic business model we all know is changing." She believes, "Leaders must be able to navigate this transition, which will be challenging. It is important for leaders to truly understand both the challenges and the opportunities that change presents, whether they are industry-wide, regulatory, legislative or customer-based."

> "The utility industry is facing uncertainty right now, and the basic business model we all know is changing."
> —Marilyn Caselli

Gregg Knight of CenterPoint Energy echoes the need for the utility business model to change. "Our business model is based on earning a return on assets. We must identify and earn a return on assets while also enhancing the delivery of service to the customer. This is GOLD."

EMPLOYEES AND TECHNOLOGY

The transformation is not limited to the industry landscape. Indeed, significant change is happening in the workforce and with technology. According to the Center for Energy Workforce Development (CEWD), the electric utility industry will need to replace almost half of its current workforce over the next decade.[1] All industries are experiencing the retirement of the baby boomer generation and the influx of the large millennial population into the workforce. From a technology perspective, customers are increasingly demanding self-service options and the technology market is exploding with connected devices, called the internet of things (IoT). The IoT is the network of physical devices, vehicles, buildings and other items—all embedded with electronics, software, sensors, actuators and network connectivity—that enable these objects to collect and exchange data.[2] Gartner research indicates that by 2020 customers will manage 85 percent of their relationship with the enterprise without interacting with a human.[3] Enabling device connectivity is exponentially increasing. Today in 2016, consumers are using over 6 billion connected devices daily. But Gartner projects that number to explode by 2020, when the IoT market is projected to include over 20 billion things.[4] These trends have implications for our workforce and our technology plans.

From a workforce perspective, SMECO's Joe Trentacosta believes, "The industry must be prepared to effectively attract and retain talent with the next generation of employees." Further Joe recommends, "Utilities must start planning now for how we as an industry are going to attract and retain the next generation of employees when their expectations are so different. They have grown up with mobile tools and devices, and everything they want is at their fingertips."

"Utilities must start planning now for how we as an industry are going to attract and retain the next generation of employees when their expectations are so different."—Joe Trentacosta

---

Marilyn Caselli agrees, "Importantly, leaders need to develop a workforce and platforms that support the new business models. New skill sets will be needed. And employees will need education and training to be prepared to meet tomorrow's energy needs."

Pointing to the changing industry, Gregg Knight calls it good news because it is attracting new employees. "A new hire in marketing," Gregg learned, "is so excited to be a part of the industry. The employee shared that the utility is the 'best place to be because I have a lot more power and influence than I realized coming into this sector.'"

The technology change also brings important challenges. Joanne Fletcher agrees, "The technology evolution is a game changer in how we serve customers." Additionally, Dave McKendry of Hydro Ottawa shares, "The explosion of the internet of things presents some tremendous opportunities to transform how we serve customers, but the challenge is the ever increasing pace of technology change." SRP's Mike Lowe notes that in addition to rising customer expectations, leaders must be aware of the rising role of technology, particularly technology beyond the meter.

"The technology evolution is a game changer in how we serve customers."—Joanne Fletcher

Joe Trentacosta comments that customers' engagements with other businesses like banks and credit card companies are setting their expectations for utility service. "For example," he says, "Customers today can take a photo using their smart phone of a check for deposit into their bank. And when that happens these customers demand more from all with whom they do business, especially their utilities." Joe believes, "Utilities need to be prepared to deliver to a customer base that expects more, wants it all and is technically savvy." Dave McKendry also cautions about ever increasing customer demands. He recognizes, "Customers will continue to compare their utility experience to other customer experiences they have, regardless of the industry. And the implication for utility customer leaders is ensuring technology infrastructure is easy and accessible for customers to use."

This technology explosion is also introducing new market entrants. These new entrants, Dave McKendry notes, "are looking to insert themselves between the utility and our customers." Mike Lowe echoes this concern and believes utilities should be asking themselves, 'Who owns the technology?' 'Who manages it?' 'Who delivers services?'" Mike increasingly thinks about the implications of *disintermediation*, that is, giving the consumer direct access to information traditionally owned and managed by the utility. The risk of not thinking through the implications of this emerging marketplace dynamic could result in a third party replacing the utility's position as the trusted energy provider.

"Utilities should be asking themselves, 'Who owns the technology?' 'Who manages it?' 'Who delivers services?'"—Mike Lowe

CUSTOMER

Joe Trentacosta highlights, "Utilities must be able to service a much more engaged and well-informed customer base and do so on the customers' terms," which are sometimes at odds with the traditional utility customer experience model. "We must engage them when they want, how they want and where they want," he continues. Referring to the transformation of the customer, he concludes, "Every year that goes by our customers become more involved and informed."

PGE's Carol Dillin sees the transformation with customers as a call to action for utilities to connect with customers as partners. She explains, "It is so interesting; a lot of our customers are calling on us to partner with them. We have large customers that want to essentially build large solar power plants and integrate to the electric system." Further, Carol recognizes a lot of customer confusion in the marketplace. "Customers are asking about micro grids but do not understand this substructure. These situations raise questions like how do we support them and ensure they have power during storms." She emphasizes, "One model will not work everywhere; different parts of country require different approaches."

Carol continues, "Right now at PGE, customers want more opportunity for green power, particularly large commercial and industrial customers who want to advertise their green ethos. Schools want solar on rooftops. And businesses want wind turbines so customers can see their active engagement in sustainable energy solutions. Developing relationship is important and it provides opportunity to create loyalty. Our customers look to us to work with them on projects as partners."

"Developing relationship is important and it provides opportunity to create loyalty. Our customers look to us to work with them on projects as partners."
—Carol Dillin

Gregg Knight believes utilities must shift their paradigm in how they engage customers to an 'outside-in approach.' He advises utility leaders, "Think about what customers need. Get in line with what they value and their value systems. We say, "Customers value their time, money and their customer experience." We (the industry) do have the power to change and transform, but it requires a framework and mindset to work in service with our customers. Utilities are service companies."

"We (the industry) do have the power to change and transform, but it requires a framework and mindset to work in service with our customers. Utilities are service companies."—Gregg Knight

---

As Greg Dunlap of PSE&G looks to the future, he believes the big challenge will be in understanding and meeting the changing expectations of customers. Increasingly, customers are not comparing utilities to other utilities, but rather they compare utilities to the best service providers out there. "We know who they are, and we know that unless we meet those expectations, we are going to lose a tremendous advantage." Greg advises utilities to concentrate on relationships, indeed partnerships, with customers. "These," he stresses, "must be cherished and held fast."

Greg advises utilities to leverage their unique position as partners with government leaders and regulators. Because of the regulatory environment, utilities are positioned to offer services for customers which others cannot. A great example of this is energy efficiency and renewables. Greg continues, "We are able to provide these services, which are highly valued by the customer, and we can do so in a manner that makes sense for us, regulators and, most importantly, the customers we serve. We must always seek and advocate for a solid regulatory framework that is to everyone's benefit."

"These (relationships with customers) must be cherished and held fast."—Greg Dunlap

---

The concurrent transformation happening with the utility industry, technology, employees and customers presents an exciting but constantly challenging environment. All these CCOs are spending significant time discerning these changes and their customer service implications. These leaders want to position their utilities to continually provide customers with highly satisfying service. The only way to do that is to understand these upcoming changes and prepare for them today. As Dave McKendry succinctly noted, "There is an ongoing need to implement customer solutions even before our customers think of them."

These are very exciting times to be in utility customer service. Upcoming leaders will be involved in developing and implementing new business and technology solutions that customers will value in this new, more complicated industry landscape. There will be increased need to educate and support customers as the industry adopts more complex solutions. Electric, gas and water customer service leaders will be challenged and rewarded for developing highly-valued customer solutions that increase goodwill to their utility. Chief Customer Officers will be the change agents helping utilities navigate these changes, adapting processes and continually serving customers with a positive, effective experience.

"There is an ongoing need to implement customer solutions even before our customers think of them."
—Dave McKendry

REFERENCES

1.   "Gaps in the Energy Workforce Pipeline 2013 Survey Results;" Center for Energy Workforce Development; www.cewd.org/documents/2013CEWDsurveyexecutivesummary.pdf.

2.   Wikipedia. En.m.wikipedia.org. "Internet of Things Global Standards Initiative." ITU. Retrieved, June 26, 2015.

3.   "Gartner Customer 360 Summit 2011" brochure; https://www.gartner.com/imagesrv/summits/docs/na/customer-360/C360_2011_brochure_FINAL.pdf

4.   www.informationweek.com/mobile/mobile-devices/gartner-21-billion-iot-devices-to-invade-by-2020.

AUTHOR'S BIOGRAPHY

Penni McLean-Conner is Chief Customer Officer and Senior Vice President of the Customer Group at Eversource Energy (NYSE: ES), the largest energy utility in New England which transmits and delivers electricity and natural gas for more than 3.6 million electric and natural gas customers in Connecticut, Massachusetts and New Hampshire.

Beginning her career as a junior engineer at Duke Power (now Duke Energy), Ms. McLean-Conner worked in Distribution Engineering, both in the field and corporate organizations until an opportunity was presented by Duke Power's first female vice president, Sharon Decker,[1] to support the establishment of a centralized customer service center. Responsible for after hour and weekend call center operations and centralized field dispatch management, Ms. McLean-Conner leveraged her engineering background and became part of an amazing transition from face-to-face customer service at nearly one hundred business offices to a 24/7 call center that offered customers self-service through the IVR. While more commonplace today, offering 24-hour customer services was a model for the utility industry.[2]

Building on the strength of her experience at Duke, Ms. McLean-Conner relocated to serve as Director of Customer Service at Tampa

Electric Company, a utility with 500,000 electric and gas customers. The hallmark of her time at TECO was re-engineering former face-to-face processes to instead provide customers with complete service options via phone. These efforts facilitated the eventual closure of all in-person customer service offices, reduced overall costs and dramatically improved J.D. Power rankings in both categories of customer service and billing and payment.

Ms. McLean-Conner affectionately recalls 2002 as 'her year of change.' Offered the opportunity to join NSTAR's executive team as the vice president of customer care and serve a much larger customer base of over 1.5 million gas and electric customers, she moved from Florida to Boston. If moving and a new job weren't rewarding enough, Ms. McLean Conner was also a newlywed and excitedly welcomed the birth of her first son, McLean during this eventful year.

During the next decade, Ms. McLean-Conner would lead initiatives that transformed service for NSTAR customers at a time when their expectations were rising for self-service options and a value-added relationship with their utility. Central to enhancing the customer experience was the introduction of a new bill with a simplified format and usage information. Additionally, the natural language interactive voice response system and enhanced web offered customers welcomed self-service. Investments in automated meter reading improved billing accuracy while reducing costs, and the implementation of a customer relationship management system supported more personalized communication with customers.

When NSTAR merged with Northeast Utilities in 2012, Ms. McLean-Conner was named to the newly created role, Chief Customer Officer, and charged with leading a team that serves over 3.5 million customers. Today as CCO and SVP, she is responsible for providing high quality customer service and delivering a cost-effective portfolio of electric and gas energy efficiency programs.

In 2015, the six brand names previously operated individually under Northeast Utilities and the six different marketplace brand promises associated with each name were merged to become one company known as Eversource Energy. Ms. McLean-Conner led, with the CEO, a successful effort to transform the customer experience, with rebranding being foundational to Eversource's mission of 'one company committed to delivering reliable energy and superior customer service.'

Demonstrating a commitment to continuous improvement, a core tenant of the combined company's brand promise, Ms. McLean-Conner has been a leader in designing and implementing "Customer Experience by Design," which focuses on the intentional – processes, systems, programs and experiences, all aimed at meeting and surpassing customer expectations. During her tenure, she has led a broad portfolio of enterprise initiatives designed to enhance the customer experience, including re-engineering the web and mobile customer interface, automating meter reading and redesigning the billing and payment process.

Ms. McLean-Conner leads Eversource's nationally recognized energy efficiency programs, saving customers nearly $1 billion on energy costs by offering customers valued solutions to use energy wisely. The Eversource Energy efficiency programs are ranked first in the nation by Ceres in their 2016 Benchmarking of Utility Clean Energy Deployment.

A recognized thought leader in the utility industry, Ms. McLean-Conner is a sought after speaker at conferences and an accomplished author. For more than seven years, she has been a featured customer service columnist for *Electric Light and Power* magazine. She has previously published two books, *Customer Service: Utility Style* and *Energy Efficiency: Principles and Practices*.

She is active in the energy industry on a national scale, serving as a member of the Edison Electric Institute Retail Services Committee, chairing the CS Week Board of Directors and presiding as president of the American Council for an Energy Efficient Economy, organizations dedicated to advancing the energy industry in customer service and energy efficiency. Ms. McLean-Conner is also active regionally and locally, serving on the Customer Advisory Council for the Fraunofer Center for Sustainable Energy Systems, the City of Boston's Green Ribbon Commission and her own town's energy committee. Her work in the industry was recently recognized by the New England Women in Energy and the Environment with their 2016 Achievement Award. One of only four honorees, Ms. McLean-Conner is a recognized trailblazer for women in the energy and environmental professions, supporting their advancement and championing diversity and inclusion programs.

Involved with various charitable organizations, Ms. McLean-Conner chairs the signature Gala for Boston's ABCD, a non-profit human services organization and serves on the Board of Directors for United Way of Massachusetts Bay. She holds a bachelor's degree in industrial engineering from North Carolina State University and is a registered Professional Engineer.

Penni McLean-Conner lives in Massachusetts with her husband Nick, and two sons McLean and Tyler. When asked what mom does for a living, McLean and Tyler are likely to say, 'She makes sure the power is on.' A busy, involved and tremendously productive leader, Ms. McLean-Conner's story is worth telling as well.

REFERENCES

1.   Sharon Decker biography; https://www.kossresource.com/sharondecker?page=0%2C1.

2.   Ibid.

INDEX

A

Action for Boston Community Development (ABCD), 196
advanced metering infrastructure (AMI), 7, 16, 33, 81, 94, 156, 157, 158, 159, 171
Amazon, 40, 103
American Bar Association, 153
    ABANet, 153
American Council for an Energy Efficient Economy, 195
American Customer Satisfaction Index®, 98
American Gas Association (AGA), 68, 186
American Public Power Association (APPA), 81
American Water Works Association, 186
Amtrak Coast Starlight, 130
Android, 32
Applause Blog (Con Edison), 9, 10, 20
Aquino, Sean, 78, 95
Arizona (AZ), 10, 121, 124, 125, 130
Arizona State University, 135
Arnold, Todd, xviii
Australia, 153, 176
automated call distribution (ACD), 86, 92
automated clearing house (ACH), 181
automated meter reading (AMR), 93, 194

B

Baby Boomer generation, 187
Bachelor of Arts (BA), 29, 135, 152, 196
Baker, David, 98, 191, 119
Baltimore, MD, 175
Bedminster, NJ, 175
Bell Atlantic Mobile, 175
Bell Canada, 152, 153, 154, 155
Bell Canada International, 153
Bell, Chip R., x, xv, 7
Bensonhurst, NY, 30
Bergen County Freeholder, 71
Bergen, Jane, xvii, 56, 58, 76
Blackwell, Johnny, 98, 100, 119
Bliss, Jeanne, 1
Bonsall, Mark, 126, 136
Boston, MA, 194, 195, 196
Branson, Richard, ix
Bring Your Own Thermostat program (PGE), 52
Brooklyn-ese, 30
Brooks, Arden, 155
Burbank, CA, 81, 94
Burbank Water and Power (BWP), v, 4, 8, 77-95, 186
Business Council for Sustainable Energy, 185
business process owner (BPO), 51
Business Solution Center (PSE&G), 74
Byrne, Ray, 155

C

Calabrese, Gerald "Gerry", 71
California (CA), 5, 82, 91, 110
California State University, Stanislaus, 135
Call Center Week, 114, 119
Call Center Week Excellence Awards, 114, 119
Calvert County, MD, 167

Canadian Bar Association, 152
CBANet, 152
Canadian Electricity Association's Customer Council, 162
Carleton University, 152
Caselli, Marilyn, v, xv, 4, 5, 9, 10, 13-34, 186, 187, 188
Castillo, Renee, xvii
Center for Energy Workforce Development (CEWD), 187, 192
CenterPoint Energy, v, xvii, 4, 8, 10, 11, 97-119, 198
Ceres' Benchmarking of Utility Clean Energy Deployment, 195
Changed Communications, xvi
Charles, Richard (Rich), xi, xiii
Charlotte, NC, vii, viii, xii, xviii
Chartwell, 67, 115
Chartwell Best Practices Award for Outage Communications, 115, 119, 160
Chernobyl, xii
chief customer officer (CCO), i, v, ix, xi, xii, xiii, xvi, 1, 3, 4, 5, 6, 7, 8, 12, 38, 121, 126, 185, 192, 193, 194
Chief Customer Officer Council (CCO Council), 1, 12
chief executive officer (CEO), vii, ix, xvi, 17, 21, 30, 48, 101, 102, 126, 130, 147, 150, 174, 176, 177, 186, 195
chief operating officer (COO), 66, 71
CIS Users Groups Conference, 3
CIS Week, 3
City of Boston Green Ribbon Commission, 195
City of Pasadena, CA, 82
Cogent Reports™, 56, 98
Collins, Lisa, xvi
Colorado (CO), 82
commercial driver's license (CDL), 131
Community Action Program, 109
compact fluorescent lights (CFL), 159
computer telephony integration (CTI), 109, 110, 116, 178
Conklin, Jeff, 2
Connecticut (CT), 193
Conner, McLean, iii, xv, 194, 196

Conner, Nick, xv, 196

Conner, Tyler, iii, xv, 196

Conrad, Bryce, xvii, 147

Consolidated Edison Company of New York, Inc. (Con Edison), v, xvi, 4, 9, 13-34, 186

consumers, 1, 2, 3, 11, 47, 55, 56, 59, 61, 63, 64, 69, 70, 141, 187, 189

contact center representative (CCR), 168, 169, 170, 182

Continental Airlines, 104

Couric, Katie, 45

critical infrastructure protection (CIP), 171

CS Week, xi, xii, xv, xvi, xviii, 1, 3, 68, 137, 145, 162, 179

CS Week Board of Directors, xviii, 195

CS Week Executive Summit, 1

CS Week Expanding Excellence Awards, 77, 178

CS Week Publishing, ii, xvi, xviii

Customer Contact Council, 105

Customer Effort Score (CenterPoint Energy), 105

customer information system (CIS), 3, 11, 24, 31, 32, 44, 50, 77, 86, 92, 93, 94, 111, 114, 157, 171, 172, 176, 177, 182

customer experience (CX), x, xvi, xvii, 2, 3, 6, 7, 8, 11, 14, 16, 17, 18, 19, 21, 33, 35, 39, 40, 41, 43, 44, 49, 50, 51, 55, 56, 57, 58, 59, 60, 61, 62, 66, 68, 69, 72, 76, 78, 90, 91, 99, 100, 101, 102, 103, 104, 106, 113, 114, 115, 118, 122, 123, 124, 127, 128, 143, 144, 146, 147, 148, 151, 156, 158, 161, 163, 164, 170, 189, 190, 191, 194, 195

Customer Experience Advisory Council (PSE&G), 66

Customer Experience by Design, 40, 195

Customer Experience Intent Statement (PGE), 50, 51

Customer Experience Roadmap (Hydro Ottawa), 148

Customer Experience Steering Committee (CxSC) (Hydro Ottawa), 148, 158

customer listening posts, 57, 58, 59, 64

Customer Operations 9-Block Grid Rating (CenterPoint Energy), 112, 113

customer relationship management (CRM), 114, 194

customer service representative (CSR), 13, 14, 27, 51, 52, 74, 89, 91, 133, 167, 171, 172

Customer Service: Utility Style, 195
Customer Touchpoints Project (PGE), 50
Customer Vision Program (CVP) (CenterPoint Energy), 101, 103

D

Daulton, Sue, xviii
Davis, Ron, xvii, 9, 77, 78, 79, 81, 84, 90, 92, 95
Davis, Kathy, 78, 95
Decker, Sharon, ix, 193, 196
Dedolf, Carter, 108, 109
Deming, Edward, viii
Digital Customer Experience (DCX) project (Con Edison), 16, 17, 21, 32
Digital Equipment Corporation PDP 11-70, 135
Dillin, Carol, v, xvi, 4, 5, 8, 35-54, 190
Dillin, Jack, xvii, 45, 46
Dippon, Dan, 98, 101, 119
disintermediation, 189
District of Columbia (DC), 70, 146, 167, 175
Dixon, Matthew, 105, 119
Donovan, Troy, 99, 100, 119
Duke Energy, ix, 193
Duke Power, vii, ix, xv, 193
Dunlap, Dr. Cherylann, xvii, 55
Dunlap, Chuck, 55
Dunlap, Gregory (Greg), v, xvii, 4, 5, 7, 55-76, 191
Dunlap, Shaun, 55
DuPont, Alexia, xvii
Duvall, Jerry, xviii

E

E. and J. Gallo Winery, 5, 135
Edison Electric Institute (EEI), 53, 68
Edison Electric Institute Retail Services Committee, 195

The Effortless Experience, 105, 119
Electric Light and Power, 56, 195
Electric Power Research Institute (EPRI), 137
electronic billing (ebill) platform, 22, 91, 92, 169, 180
Ellis, Kathleen, 71
EnergE Link, 74, 75
Energy Central, 111
energy efficiency (EE), 53, 61, 64, 75, 159, 191, 194, 195
Energy Efficiency Programs (CenterPoint Energy), 108
Energy Efficiency: Principles and Practices
Energy Strong (PSE&G), 63, 76
Enhancing Customer Relationships (ECR) Team (Con Edison), 14
engaged customer relations (ECR) scores, 56
Ernst and Young (EY), xi
Esler, Patricia (Patti), xvii, 66, 72
E-Source, 67
Eugene, OR, 35
Eversource Energy, xi, xvi, 67, 193, 195
Executive Order 7037, 167
EZ-3 (SRP time-of-use tariff option), 139, 140, 141

F

Facebook, 173, 180
Fadriquela, Nancy, 78, 95
Fairleigh Dickinson University, 69
Financial World, vii
First call resolution, 9, 90, 91, 158, 170
Fletcher, Joanne, v, xvii, 4, 5, 8, 9, 10, 77-95, 186, 188, 189
Flores, Joe, 78, 95
Florida (FL), 194
Forline, Joe, xvii, 57, 58, 62, 71, 76
Fortune, vii
Fowler, Peggy, 48
Fox, Larry, 152, 155
Fraunofer Center for Sustainable Energy Systems, Customer
    Advisory Council, 195
Fraser, Norm, xvii, 143, 144, 162

G

Gallo, Christopher, xvi
Gardiner, Tami, 164, 183
Gartner, 187, 192
General Electric (GE), 110
geographic information system (GIS), 182
Gloucester Hydro, 146
Google, 3, 53, 103, 116
Goulbourn Hydro, 146
Grabinski, Janet, xvi
green power, 38, 67, 190
Greg Green (Hydro Ottawa persona), 160

H

Harvard Business School, ix
Hayes, Gary, 113
Heilbrunn, Leslie, 36, 38, 54
Hernandez, Ozzie, 78, 95
Home Service Plus® (HSP) (CenterPoint Energy), 109, 111
Hoover Dam, 81
Hou, Tim, 78, 95
Houston Gas Light Company, 102
Houston, TX, 102, 104, 112
Hurricane Hugo, viii
Hurricane Irene, 63
Hydro Ottawa, v, xvii, 4, 143-162, 188

I

IBM's 'Design Thinking,' 117
Idaho (ID), 46
IKON Office Solutions, 110
iNET2000, 152
information technology (IT), 31, 66, 72, 123, 128, 129, 135, 163, 164, 174, 175

Intelligent Utility, 111
Intended Customer Experience (PGE), 41
intentional customer experience, 40, 41, 43
interactive voice response (IVR), 11, 23, 47, 51, 52, 86, 92, 106, 107, 114, 115, 116, 118, 133, 160, 179, 193, 194
internal compliance program (ICP), 171
International Brotherhood of Electrical Workers, Local 266, 131
internet of things (IoT), 130, 162, 187, 188, 192
iPhone Operating System (iOS), 32, 53
Issues Team (SRP), 132

J

Jacobson, Lisa, 185
J.D. Power, 2, 40, 53, 55, 58, 59, 60, 64, 65, 68, 75, 91, 121, 132, 150, 163, 179, 180, 183, 194
J.D. Power Business Gas customer satisfaction award, 75
J.D. Power Business Electric customer satisfaction award, 75
J.D. Power Electric Utility Residential Customer Satisfaction Trend, 2, 64
Johnson, Karen, xvii

K

Kaczmarek, Teri, 78, 90, 95
Kanata Hydro, 146
Kantor, Rosabeth Moss, ix
Kelly, Mike, xvii
Key Middle School, 112
key performance indicators (KPIs), 7, 21, 58, 173
"The Killer B's and All About Me," 11, 145, 157, 158, 159
KITE Award, 111
Knight, Gregory (Gregg), v, xvii, 4, 5, 8, 10, 97-119, 187, 188, 190, 191
Koeppe, Al, 71
Korenek, Debbie, 99, 100, 119
Kulkarni, Kapil, 78, 79, 95

L

Landau, Caroline, xvi
LaRossa, Ralph, 66
Las Vegas, NV, 46
Lee III, William States (Bill), vii-x
Lewis, Bill, 82
light emoting diode (LED) lights, 159
Litke, Rod, xvi, xviii, 145
Los Angeles, CA, 130
Lowe, Michael (Mike), v, xvii, 4, 5, 7, 10, 121-142, 188, 189
Lucas, Anna, xvii

M

management information system (MIS), 174
"man on the street" videos, 37
Market Strategies International (MSI), 2, 3, 56, 59, 64, 73, 75
Market Strategies Utility Trusted Brand and Customer Engagement
    study, 3
Marketing Executive Council, 137
Massachusetts (MA), 193, 196
Master of Business Administration (MBA), 48, 135
Master of Public Administration (MPA), 82
McAvoy, John, 17, 18
McCurdy, Dave, 186
McDonald, Marybeth, 162
McGoldrick, Joe, 99, 101, 119
MCI, 109, 110, 111
McKendry, Allie, 152
McKendry, Chelsea, 152
McKendry, David (Dave), 152, 153
McKendry, Karen, 152, 153
McKendry, Matt, 152
McLean-Conner, Penni, i, ii, ix, 34, 54, 76, 95, 119, 142, 162, 183,
    193-196
Mendonca, Michael, xvii, 122, 142

meter data management (MDM), 44, 50, 86, 92, 93, 114, 171
Metro Mobile, 175
Meyer, Jeanette, 78, 80, 95
MG-Strategy, 19
millennials, 98, 117, 118, 187
Minister of the Word and Sacrament, 71
Minnesota (MN), 102, 108
Minneapolis, MN, 102
Minneapolis Gas Light Company, 102
Mississippi River, 102
Modesto, CA, 135
'moment of truth,' 58, 59, 75
My conEdison (Con Edison), 32
MyHydroLink (MHL) (Hydro Ottawa), 145, 158, 159, 160, 161

N

Nash, Bill, xvii, 57, 76
National Football League, 97
National Reclamation Act, 145
Natural Gas Utilities Playbook, 186
Navajo Indian Reservation, 125
Nepean Hydro, 146
NEST, 11, 49, 52, 53
New England Women in Energy and the Environment (NEWIEE)
    Environment Achievement Award, 196
New Hampshire (NH), 193
New Jersey (NJ), 7, 55, 56, 63, 70, 175
New Jersey Natural Gas, 71
New York City, NY, 13, 17, 24, 30, 175
New York Stock Exchange (NYSE), 48, 193
New York Times, xv, 7
New Zealand, 153
Nicholson, Bill, 36, 54
North America,
North American Electric Reliability Corporation (NERC) CIP
    (Critical Infrastructure Protection), 171

North American Electric Reliability Corporation (NERC) ICP (Internal Compliance Program), 171
North Bergen, NJ, 55
North Carolina State University, 196
Northeast Utilities, 194
Norton, Margaret, xvi
NSTAR, 194
nuclear plant, vii, 46

O

Oberle, Chris, 3
O'Connor, Jerry, 71
Ottawa, Ontario, 5, 143, 145, 146, 153, 154
Ottawa Electric Company, 146
outage management system (OMS), 160, 172, 176, 180, 182
Overton, Kerry, xviii

P

PA Consulting, 55
Paul, Elizabeth, 36, 38, 54
Peck, Charles, 78, 90, 95
Pelt-Thornton, Andrea, xviii
Penny Pinched (Hydro Ottawa persona), 149, 160
personal identification number (PIN), 181
Phoenix, AZ, 125, 130
Pickeral-Brown, Rose, 164, 166, 183
Plus One (+1) Experience (Con Edison), 19, 20, 33
Portland, OR, 35, 36, 43, 46, 53, 130
Portland General Electric (PGE), v, xvi, 4, 8, 35-54
Power Alert Service® (PAS) (CenterPoint Energy), 106, 114, 115, 116
Power Talk (PSE&G), 65
Pratt, Jim, xvii, 122, 142
pre-pay (SRP), 123, 124, 133, 138, 139
President and CEO's Award for Innovation and Productivity (Hydro Ottawa), 156

Prochazka, Scott M., 102
programmable connected thermostat (PCT), 52
prosumers, 33
Provost, Michel, xvii, 143, 145, 162
Public Service Electric and Gas (PSE&G), v, xvii, 4, 8, 55-76, 191
Public Service Enterprise Group (PSE&G), 56
The Pulse, 134

Q

Quin, David, xvii, 99, 100, 101, 119

R

Reis, Nancy, 78, 95
Reformed Church in America, 71
Reliable Public Power Provider (RP3) Award, 81
Reliant Energy, 110
Reliant Resources, 102
Renewable Portfolio Standard (BWP), 81
residential demand response program, 52, 53
Ressler, Terry, xviii
Rethinking Utility Customer Care: Satisfying Your Always-Connected, Always-On Customers, xviii
Ricoh, 110
Riverside, CA, 97
RKS Marketing Research Company (RKS), 91
Rober, Susan, xvi
Rogers, Will, ix
Roosevelt, President Franklin, 167
Rural Electrification Administration, 167
Rush Hour Rewards Pilot (PGE), 52
Rutgers University School of Engineering, 69, 71

S

Sarkissian, Arineh, 79, 95

Salt River, 125

Salt River Project (SRP), v, xvii, 4, 7, 10, 121-142, 188

Salt River Valley, 125

Salt River Valley Water Users' Association, 125

Sam Simplify (Hydro Ottawa persona), 149, 160

Sawchuk, Corey, xvi

Sawchuk, Craig, xvi

scorecard, 59, 66, 67, 72, 178

senior vice president (SVP), 3, 4, 8, 14, 23, 28, 36, 98, 111, 163, 174,
    177, 193, 194

Sherman, TX, i, ii

Silberman College of Business, 69

Singapore, 153, 154

Siri, 116

Six Sigma, 101, 110

Slater, Joe, xviii, 164, 165, 166, 176, 177, 183

smart grid, 7, 63, 79, 80, 81, 93, 113

Southern Maryland Electric Cooperative (SMECO), v, 4, 8, 9, 163-
    183, 188

Southern Maryland Tri-County Cooperative Association, 167

speech analytics, 9, 171, 179, 181, 182

Stassi, Ron, 83, 84

State of the Water Industry Report, 186

State University of New York (SUNY), Empire State College, 29

Stay Safe, Stay Warm program (CenterPoint Energy), 128

Success Sciences, 19

succession planning, 49, 72, 90, 157

Superstorm Sandy, 63

supervisory control and data acquisition (SCADA), 176

Swanson, Heidi, xvii, 57, 58, 59, 76

Sydney, Australia, 155

T

Tampa Electric Company (TECO), 193, 194
Team Building Committee (BWP), 83
Texas (TX), 102, 110
Texas Genco, 102
Theodore Roosevelt Dam, 125
Three Mile Island, vii
time-of-use (TOU), 138, 139, 140, 141, 156, 158, 159
Tonto Basin, 125
Toronto, Ontario, 152
Town of Casselman, 146
Traasdahl, Glen, xvii, 122, 123, 124, 142
Transforming the Customer Experience (TCX) Awards (Con
    Edison), 20
Trentacosta, Joseph (Joe), v, xviii, 4, 5, 8, 163-183, 188, 189, 190
Trentacosta, Mary, xviii, 175
Trenton, NJ, 70
Twitter, 22, 23, 180

U

Uber, 40
United Airlines, 104
United Way, 145
Revenue Management Committee, 145
United Way of Massachusetts Bay, 196
University of Colorado, 97
US Supreme Court, 153
Utility Bill (BWP), 83
Utility Dive, 67
Utility Workers Union of America, AFL-CIO, Local 601, 71
Utility Workers Union of America, Locals 1-2 and 3, 27

V

Verizon, 109
Viar, Dave, 164, 183
Virgin Group, ix
Virginia (VA), 153
voice of the customer (VoC), 6, 9, 10, 14, 17, 18, 21, 26, 31, 33, 39, 42, 43, 57, 58, 64, 66, 73, 100, 105, 106, 114, 126, 129, 130, 132, 148, 150, 151, 170, 173

W

Watson, Burke, xvii
The Way We Work (Con Edison), 27, 34
Welch, Sylvia, 164, 166, 183
Westchester County (NY), 17
Wisdom, Wayne, xvii, 123, 142
Woodcliff Community Reformed Church, 71
Word cloud,
    Marilyn Caselli word cloud, 15
    Carol Dillin word cloud, 37
    Greg Dunlap word cloud, 57
    Joanne Fletcher word cloud, 78
    Gregg Knight word cloud, 90
    Mike Lowe word cloud, 122
    Dave McKendry word cloud 144
    Omni word cloud, 6
    Joe Trentacosta word cloud, 165
World Association of Nuclear Operators, vii
WorldCom, 110
Wyatt, Mark, xviii

X – Y – Z

York University, 152
Zappos, 103
Zittle, Cheryl, xviii, 123, 124, 142

CPSIA information can be obtained
at www.ICGtesting.com
Printed in the USA
BVOW06*1726031116

466806BV00002B/3/P